Greg Sanders, Advocate, has been involved in numerous property cases since calling to the Scottish Bar in 2001. These have included Right to Roam cases acting for Landowners and Ramblers. Greg's property practice has included being instructed as a skilled witness for the High Court in England (relating to Scottish servitude rights (easements).

A Practical Guide to
the Right to Roam
in Scotland

A Practical Guide to the Right to Roam in Scotland

Greg Sanders,

Advocate,

Westwater Advocates,

Faculty of Advocates,

Parliament House,

Edinburgh,

EH1 1RF

Law Brief Publishing

Published 2023 by Law Brief Publishing, an imprint of Law Brief Publishing Ltd
30 The Parks
Minehead
Somerset
TA24 8BT

www.lawbriefpublishing.com

Paperback: 978-1-914608-67-4

This book is dedicated to Scotland's Adders

PREFACE

There are several excellent textbooks that deal with the "Right to Roam" Provisions, Part 1, of the Land Reform (Scotland) Act 2003. This book is intended to be a practical guide for Lawyers, Land Owners, Visitors and those authorised to enforce the 2003 Act.

Rather than being a theoretical text this is a practical guide to the subject. It is intended to enable readers to grasp the subject quickly and, if necessary, litigate. It includes style Summary Application proceedings by way of guidance.

The stated law is believed to be correct as at January 31st 2023.

Greg Sanders
Advocate
Westwater Advocates
January 2023

CONTENTS

CONTENTS

CHAPTER ONE

INTRODUCTION

This is intended to be a practical guide to the "Right to Roam" in Scotland. It is therefore restricted to the provisions of Part 1 of the Land Reform (Scotland) Act 2003 ("the 2003 Act"). It is intended to be of practical use to landowners, local authorities, ramblers (visitors) and all of those with an interest in access rights to land. It does not discuss public rights of way or servitudes (easements).

There is necessary (and hopefully interesting) discussion of the applicable law, how best to avoid disputes, how to be considerate to farmers, how to resolve disputes and, if all else fails, how to litigate disputes. This is all hopefully explained in a way that is understandable to those that may not have a legal background.

Litigation should be avoided if at all possible. Litigating these cases is expensive even for the successful party. In Scotland, and as a general rule of thumb, the successful party will, at best, only recover 50%-55% of actual expenses incurred in pursuing or defending an action in the Sheriff Court. The words "it's a matter of principle" are mellifluous to a litigation lawyer.

Those looking for more detailed or theoretical reading are referred to:

(i)   Professor R.R.M Paisley's 2006 "Access Rights and Rights of Way: A Guide to the Law in Scotland";

(ii) Chapter 27 of Gordon and Wortley's Scottish Land Law (Third Edition Volume 2);

(iii) The Scot Ways Guide to The Law of Access to Land in Scotland (2018) Ch.2; and

(iv) Gloag and Henderson, The Law of Scotland, Fifteenth Edition Volume II at 34.113 onwards.

Those that are time constrained should read:

(i) Part 1 of the 2003 Act; and

(ii) Anstalt v Loch Lomond and Trossachs National Park Authority [2018] CSIH 22.

These cover most of what is realistically likely to arise in relation to part 1 of the 2003 Act.

CHAPTER TWO

DEFINITIONS AND
TERMINOLOGY

There is limited utility in reading through the chapters of this book without understanding the terminology. Readers are therefore referred to section 32 being the last section in part 1 of the 2003 Act.

"32 Interpretation of Part 1

In this Part of this Act—

"Access Code" means the Scottish Outdoor Access Code issued by Scottish Natural Heritage under section 10.....;

"canals" means inland waterways within the meaning of section 92 (interpretation) of the Transport Act 1962 (c. 46);

"core path" means a path, waterway or any other means of crossing land such as is mentioned in section 17(2) above which is set out in a plan adopted under section 18 above or, as the case may be, such a plan as amended under section 20 above;

"cultural heritage" includes structures and other remains resulting from human activity of all periods, traditions, ways of life and the historic, artistic and literary associations of people, places and landscapes;

"inland waters" means any inland, non-tidal loch, river (to the extent that it is non-tidal), lake or reservoir, whether natural or artificial and whether navigable or not, and includes the bed and the shores or banks thereof;

"land" includes—

(a) *bridges and other structures built on or over land;*

(b) *inland waters;*

(c) *canals; and*

(d) *the foreshore, that is to say, the land between the high and low water marks of ordinary spring tides;*

"local authority" in relation to specific land in respect of which access rights are or would, but for a provision of or order made under this Act, be exercisable means—

(a) *where the land is, on the day on which this section comes into force, within an area designated as a National Park under the National Parks (Scotland) Act 2000 (asp 10), the National Park authority for that National Park; and*

(b) *in any other case, the council (being a council constituted under section 2 of the Local Government etc. (Scotland) Act 1994 (c. 39)) whose area includes that land;*

"natural heritage" includes the flora and fauna of land, its geological and physiographical features and its natural beauty and amenity;

"owner", in relation to land, means—

(a) *the owner of the land; and*

(b) *where the owner is not in natural possession of the land, the person who is entitled to such natural possession;*

"statutory undertaker" means—

(a) a person authorised by any enactment to carry on any railway, light railway, tramway, road transport, water transport, canal, inland navigation, dock, harbour, pier or lighthouse undertaking or any undertaking for the supply of hydraulic power;

(b) the operator of a electronic communications code network;

(c) an airport operator (within the meaning of the Airports Act 1986 (c. 31)) operating an airport to which Part V of that Act applies;

(d) a gas transporter, within the meaning of Part I of the Gas Act 1986 (c. 44);

(e) Scottish Water;

(f) a holder of a licence under section 6(1) of the Electricity Act 1989 (c. 29);

(g) the Civil Aviation Authority or a holder of a licence under Chapter I of Part I of the Transport Act 2000 (c. 38) (to the extent that the person holding the licence is carrying out activities authorised by it);

(h) the Scottish Environment Protection Agency; or

(i) a universal service provider within the meaning of Part 3 of the Postal Services Act 2011 (c.5)];

and "undertaking" means the undertaking of such a statutory undertaker

. . . . "

CHAPTER THREE

ACCESS RIGHTS

Pre 2003

Pre 2003 there was perhaps an incorrect perception that there was no law of trespass in Scotland. There remains statutory (criminal) and common law trespass (civil) trespass.

Criminal

In relation to statutory trespass section 3(1) of the Trespass (Scotland) Act 1865 provides:

> *"Every person who lodges in any premises, or occupies or encamps on any land, being private property, without the consent and permission of the owner or legal occupier of such premises or land, and every person who encamps or lights a fire on or near any . . . road or enclosed or cultivated land, or in or near any plantation, without the consent and permission of the owner or legal occupier of such road, land, or plantation . . . shall be guilty of an offence punishable as herein-after provided."*

The foregoing sometimes led to acrimony between land owners and "visitors" being asked to leave private property failing which the owner would threaten to involve the police. There are no reported cases of prosecutions under the 1865 Act. This is not surprising given that section 4 of the 1865 Act provides:

> *"A person committing an offence against the provisions of this Act shall be liable, on summary conviction, to a fine not exceeding level 1 on the standard scale."*

After more than 150 years it is even less likely that there will be any imminent test cases under the 1865 Act. Section 3(2) of the 1865 Act was inserted by the 2003 Act and qualified matters:

> *"Subsection (1) above does not extend to anything done by a person in the exercise of the access rights created by the Land Reform (Scotland) Act 2003.."*

The 1865 Act accordingly remains in force.

Civil

There remains common law trespass; Walker's Civil Remedies, at page 957, discusses this. A land owner is entitled to exclusive lawful possession of his property and in certain limited circumstances can sue for recoverable losses caused by a trespasser. In reality, if aggrieved, an owner would simply ask a trespasser to leave.

2003 Act

Since 9th February 2005 section 1 of the 2003 Act ensured that everyone has access rights (a statutory right to roam). This right encompasses access for recreational, educational and for limited commercial purposes. Limited commercial purposes might include someone taking photographs or operating a drone.

The right to roam is a right to go into, over, above, below and remaining on land. It can be a combination of all these (e.g. camping). The statutory right is in addition to common law rights of access such as public rights of way or, discussed elsewhere, core paths.

Section 1 is as follows:

1. Access rights

(1) Everyone has the statutory rights established by this Part of this Act.

(2) Those rights (in this Part of this Act called "access rights") are—

    (a) the right to be, for any of the purposes set out in subsection (3) below, on land; and

    (b) the right to cross land.

(3) The right set out in subsection (2)(a) above may be exercised only

    (a) for recreational purposes;

    (b) for the purposes of carrying on a relevant educational activity; or

    (c) for the purposes of carrying on, commercially or for profit, an activity which the person exercising the right could carry on otherwise than commercially or for profit.

(4) The reference—

    (a) in subsection (2)(a) above to being on land for any of the purposes set out in subsection (3) above is a reference to—

        (i) going into, passing over and remaining on it for any of those purposes and then leaving it; or

> (ii) any combination of those;
>
> (b) in subsection (2)(b) above to crossing land is a reference to going into it, passing over it and leaving it all for the purpose of getting from one place outside the land to another such place.
>
> (5) A "relevant educational activity" is, for the purposes of subsection (3) above, an activity which is carried on by a person for the purposes of—
>
> (a) furthering the person's understanding of natural or cultural heritage; or
>
> (b) enabling or assisting other persons to further their understanding of natural or cultural heritage.
>
> (6) Access rights are exercisable above and below (as well as on) the surface of the land.
>
> (7) The land in respect of which access rights are exercisable is all land except that specified in or under section 6 below.

Access Rights to be exercised responsibly

With access rights comes responsibility. Access rights must be exercised responsibly.

Section 2 provides:

> "2. Access rights to be exercised responsibly
>
> (1) A person has access rights only if they are exercised responsibly.

(2) *In determining whether access rights are exercised responsibly a person is to be presumed to be exercising access rights responsibly if they are exercised so as not to cause unreasonable interference with any of the rights (whether access rights, rights associated with the ownership of land or any others) of any other person, but—*

    (a) *a person purporting to exercise access rights who, at the same time—*

        (i) *engages in any of the conduct within section 9 below or within any byelaw made under section 12(1)(a)(i) below; or*

        (ii) *does anything which undoes anything done by Scottish Natural Heritage under section 29 below,*

    is to be taken as not exercising those rights responsibly; and

    (b) *regard is to be had to whether the person exercising or purporting to exercise access rights is, at the same time—*

        (i) *disregarding the guidance on responsible conduct set out in the Access Code and incumbent on persons exercising access rights; or*

        (ii) *disregarding any request included or which might reasonably be implied in anything done by Scottish Natural Heritage under section 29 below.*

(3) In this section the references to the responsible exercise of access rights are references to the exercise of these rights in a way which is lawful and reasonable and takes proper account of the interests of others and of the features of the land in respect of which the rights are exercised.

With reference to section 2 (2) (a) (i) "excluded conduct", as defined by section 9, is:

The conduct which is within this section is—

(a) being on or crossing land in breach of an interdict or other order of a court;

(b) being on or crossing land for the purpose of doing anything which is an offence or a breach of an interdict or other order of a court;

(c) hunting, shooting or fishing;

(d) being on or crossing land while responsible for a dog or other animal which is not under proper control;

(e) being on or crossing land for the purpose of taking away, for commercial purposes or for profit, anything in or on the land;

(f) being on or crossing land in or with a motorised vehicle or vessel (other than a vehicle or vessel which has been constructed or adapted for use by a person who has a disability and which is being used by such a person);

(g) being, for any of the purposes set out in section 1(3) above, on land which is a golf course.

<u>Reciprocal obligations of owners</u>

In terms of section 3 of the 2003 Act owners are under a duty to use and manage land in a way that respects and facilitates the aforementioned rights of access.

Section 3 provides:

> (1) *It is the duty of every owner of land in respect of which access rights are exercisable—*
>
> > (a) *to use and manage the land; and*
> >
> > (b) *otherwise to conduct the ownership of it,*
>
> *in a way which, as respects those rights, is responsible.*
>
> (2) *In determining whether the way in which land is used, managed or the ownership of it is conducted is responsible an owner is to be presumed to be using, managing and conducting the ownership of land in a way which is responsible if it does not cause unreasonable interference with the access rights of any person exercising or seeking to exercise them, but—*
>
> > (a) *an owner who contravenes section 14(1) or (3) or 23(2) of this Act or any byelaw made under section 12(1)(a)(ii) below is to be taken as not using, managing or conducting the ownership of the land in a responsible way;*
> >
> > (b) *regard is to be had to whether any act or omission occurring in the use, management or conduct of the ownership of the land disregards the guidance on responsible conduct set out in the Access Code and incumbent on the owners of land.*

(3) *In this section the references to the use, management and conduct of the ownership of land in a way which is responsible are references to the use, management and conduct of the ownership of it in a way which is lawful and reasonable and takes proper account of the interests of persons exercising or seeking to exercise access rights.*

Section 6 Non-exercisable rights

Certain land is excluded. Specifically, section 6 of the 2003 Act provides:

6. Land over which access rights not exercisable

(1) *The land in respect of which access rights are not exercisable is land—*

(a) *to the extent that there is on it—*

(i) *a building or other structure or works, plant or fixed machinery;*

(ii) *a caravan, tent or other place affording a person privacy or shelter;*

(b) *which—*

(i) *forms the curtilage of a building which is not a house or of a group of buildings none of which is a house;*

(ii) *forms a compound or other enclosure containing any such structure, works, plant or fixed machinery as is referred to in paragraph (a)(i) above;*

   (iii) *consists of land contiguous to and used for the purposes of a school; or*

   (iv) *comprises, in relation to a house or any of the places mentioned in paragraph (a)(ii) above, sufficient adjacent land to enable persons living there to have reasonable measures of privacy in that house or place and to ensure that their enjoyment of that house or place is not unreasonably disturbed;*

 (c) *to which, not being land within paragraph (b)(iv) above, two or more persons have rights in common and which is used by those persons as a private garden;*

 (d) *to which public access is, by or under any enactment other than this Act, prohibited, excluded or restricted;*

 (e) *which has been developed or set out—*

   (i) *as a sports or playing field; or*

   (ii) *for a particular recreational purpose;*

 (f) *to which—*

   (i) *for not fewer than 90 days in the year ending on 31st January 2001, members of the public were admitted only on payment; and*

   (ii) *after that date, and for not fewer than 90 days in each year beginning on 1st February 2001, members of the public are, or are to be, so admitted;*

(g) *on which—*

    (i) *building, civil engineering or demolition works; or*

    (ii) *works being carried out by a statutory undertaker for the purposes of the undertaking,*

are being carried out;

(h) *which is used for the working of minerals by surface workings (including quarrying);*

(i) *in which crops have been sown or are growing;*

(j) *which has been specified in an order under section 11 or in byelaws under section 12 below as land in respect of which access rights are not exercisable.*

(2) *For the purposes of subsection (1)(a)(i) above, a bridge, tunnel, causeway, launching site, groyne, weir, boulder weir, embankment of a canalised waterway, fence, wall or anything designed to facilitate passage is not to be regarded as a structure."*

Section 6 of the 2003 Act attempts to strike a balance between the interests of landowners and visitors. Section 6 does so by setting out statutory exclusions as to land that cannot be accessed. It is a contentious section being open, until recently, to creative interpretation by those attempting to exercise or restrict access. This section has given rise to a volume of litigation culminating in Anstalt. Anstalt clarifies many issues arising from the operation of section 6 of the 2003 Act and an authority exercising its section 14 enforcement rights under the 2003 Act.

CHAPTER FOUR

ENFORCEMENT OF ACCESS RIGHTS

Sections 13 and 14 of the 2003 Act give local authorities powers to carry out enforcement steps, including court proceedings, if the authority believes that a landowner is failing to comply with the 2003 Act. This usually relates to locked gates, "keep out" signs and, of course, the latest herd of wild boar ("Sus scrofa").

Sections 13 and 14 of the 2003 Act provide

13 Duty of local authority to uphold access rights

(1) *It is the duty of the local authority to assert, protect and keep open and free from obstruction or encroachment any route, waterway or other means by which access rights may reasonably be exercised.*

(2) *A local authority is not required to do anything in pursuance of the duty imposed by subsection (1) above which would be inconsistent with the carrying on of any of the authority's other functions.*

(3) *The local authority may, for the purposes set out in subsection (1) above, institute and defend legal proceedings and generally take such steps as they think expedient.*

14 Prohibition signs, obstructions, dangerous impediments etc.

(1) *The owner of land in respect of which access rights are exercisable shall not, for the purpose or for the main purpose of preventing or deterring any person entitled to exercise these rights from doing so—*

    (a) *put up any sign or notice;*

    (b) *put up any fence or wall, or plant, grow or permit to grow any hedge, tree or other vegetation;*

    (c) *position or leave at large any animal;*

    (d) *carry out any agricultural or other operation on the land; or*

    (e) *take, or fail to take, any other action.*

(2) *Where the local authority consider that anything has been done in contravention of subsection (1) above they may, by written notice served on the owner of the land, require that such remedial action as is specified in the notice be taken by the owner of the land within such reasonable time as is so specified.*

(3) *If the owner fails to comply with such a notice, the local authority may—*

    (a) *remove the sign or notice; or, as the case may be,*

    (b) *take the remedial action specified in the notice served under subsection (2) above,*

and, in either case, may recover from the owner such reasonable costs as they have incurred by acting under this subsection.

(4) *An owner on whom a notice has been so served may, by summary application made to the sheriff, appeal against it.*

(5) *Rules of Court shall provide—*

    (a) *for public notice of the making of summary applications for the purposes of this section;*

    (b) *for enabling persons interested in the exercise of access rights over the land to which a summary application relates, and persons or bodies representative of such persons, to be parties to the proceedings;*

    (c) *for limiting the number of persons and bodies who may be such parties.*

CHAPTER FIVE

SCOTTISH OUTDOOR ACCESS CODE

Section 10 of the 2003 Act provides:

10 The Scottish Outdoor Access Code

(1) It is the duty of Scottish Natural Heritage to draw up and issue a code, to be known as the Scottish Outdoor Access Code, setting out, in relation to access rights, guidance as to the circumstances in which—

(a) those exercising these rights are to be regarded as doing so in a way which is or is not responsible;

(b) persons are to be regarded as carrying on activities, otherwise than in the course of exercising access rights, in a way which is likely to affect the exercise of these rights by other persons;

(c) owners of land in respect of which these rights are exercisable are to be regarded as using and managing, or otherwise conducting the ownership of it, in a way which is or is not responsible;

(d) owners of land in respect of which these rights are not exercisable are to be regarded as using and managing, or otherwise conducting the ownership of it, in a way which is likely to affect the exercise of these rights on land which is contiguous to that land.

> *(2) Scottish Natural Heritage shall consult local authorities and such other persons or bodies as they think appropriate about the proposed Access Code and then submit it (with or without modifications) to Ministers together with copies of any objections or representations made in response to that consultation…*

The Scottish Outdoor Access Code can be found online at http://mygov.scot/Scottish-outdoor-access code. The Code is actually legislated for by section 10 of the 2003 Act. It is undoubtedly of assistance to those that know of its existence, have read it and heed it. There is a great deal of useful information on the aforesaid website.

Core themes of the code include respecting the interests of other people, caring for the environment and taking personal responsibility. On one view the Access Code does no more than state the obvious and common sense. It could be argued that the Code works relatively well given the relatively low number of litigated cases. Readers are referred to the website for parkswatchscotland for lively commentary about the efficacy of the Code and other matters concerning the 2003 Act. On another view, many taking access have no knowledge of the 2003 Act and/or the Access Code. Is the existence of the 2003 Act and the Code is even known about to those that abandon tents, disposable barbeques and have limited toilet etiquette? As commented earlier the Code was discussed in the Gloag judgment where even those with a professed knowledge of the code did not adhere to it.

Several organisations have attempted to promulgate knowledge of the code; e.g. young.scot have a "Know the Code Campaign" that addresses issues such as crossing a field with farm animals and calls of nature with no toilets in sight.

Visitors

The code stresses that when visiting the outdoors, visitors must behave responsibly, and the Code explains what this means. The main responsibilities are be summarised as –

- Taking personal responsibility care for safety, staying alert for hazards and taking special care with children. This does not conflict with Occupiers' Liability.

- Respect people's privacy and peace of mind.

- Help land managers and others to work safely and effectively – e.g. keep clear of land management operations like harvesting or tree-felling, avoid damaging crops, leave gates as they are found.

- Care for the environment – e.g. don't disturb wildlife, take litter away.

- Keep dogs under proper control – dogs are popular companions, but take special care if near livestock, or during the bird breeding season, and always pick up dog excrement. There is not, but should be, a reminder to pick up or safely bury human excrement. Errant dogs are a particular worry to farmers before and during lambing.

- Take extra care if organising an event or running a business – e.g. talk to the managers of any land which you may plan to use intensively or regularly.

<u>Owners/Managers</u>

Owners or managers of land or water in Scotland must manage that land in a way which is responsible in respect of the public's statutory access rights.

Main responsibilities are to:

- Respect access rights in managing land and water – e.g. by not hindering or deterring people, and taking access into account when planning management tasks.
- Act reasonably when asking people to avoid land management operations – e.g. by keeping any precautions to the minimum area and duration required for people's safety.
- Work with the local authority and other bodies to help integrate access and land management – e.g. show that people are welcome, work with the access officer to help manage access positively.

When managing land and water where access rights do not apply, e.g. a farmyard, must take into account neighbouring land and water where access rights do apply. People can be asked to avoid routes while certain work is going on, e.g. if work will create serious or less obvious hazards for a period (tree felling or blasting).

Notwithstanding the outdoor access code there have been reported court cases. Knowledge of the outdoor access code, whilst helpful, does not necessarily prevent such disputes coming before the courts. In this regard some of the Sheriff's *obiter* comments in Gloag supra (paragraphs 20-22) make interesting reading:

> "20. *Mr M then set off on his expedition walking round the edge of the lawn as demonstrated on the plan by him and round what has been described in the evidence as the horseshoe area to the south-west and then at some stage noticed a police car arriving in*

the back gate of the castle so he immediately began to traverse the garden area near where there is an ornamental stream, a small bridge and some cultivated flower beds towards the police officers.

The car contained two police officers who spoke to Mr M. He explained his purpose in being in the premises. He claimed to be operating in terms of the new legislation.

The police officers indicated they were aware of the existence of the legislation but did not claim to have a detailed knowledge of its terms. At some stage Mr M asked if they had a copy of the code and when they explained that they did not he proffered one for their future use explaining he had plenty of them. He informed the police officers that he was of the view that any dispute between him and the land manager was a civil dispute implying, if not specifically saying, that it had nothing to do with them, which dispute arose in terms of the new legislation.

In the meantime another police car arrived at the scene with two further police officers who joined in the discussion. It was agreed by the police officers that the matter was a civil dispute and they intended to take no action in relation to Mr M other than to request him to give them his full name and address and other details and then they made their way to the castle itself. Mr M of course was not aware of what the police officers told those in the Castle but he assumed that they told them that the matter was a civil dispute which did not concern them (the police officers). He then finished his business at the castle and made his way back across the edge of the lawn and when he arrived back at the main gate, coincidentally, the gate opened to allow others to pass through and he made his exit.

21. In some ways that evidence was rather surprising considering what Mr M had said about the majority of access takers. He had indicated that 95 per cent of such people follow the code. Yet he himself had taken access across land in the teeth of opposition by the land manager which he was acutely aware was land excluded from the right of access by the legislation and very certainly by the very document which he had handed over to police officers. Not only was he not exercising access responsibly in terms of the code he was exercising access over land which he knew was excluded from the right of access contained in the legislation in circumstances when he had specifically been requested to leave. Matters become worse, however, because when the police officers arrived, in circumstances where prior to the legislation no doubt they would have simply asked him to leave, they were informed by him that it was not a criminal matter for them but a civil matter and they fell for it, when in truth he was probably creating a breach of the peace by refusing to leave when requested to do so in circumstances where he was exercising a right of access which he knew did not exist. In short he had chosen to ignore the very legislation that he was complimenting because it suited his purpose.

22. How, then, does that affect the evidence given by both Mr M and Mr S about the effectiveness of the law in protecting the rights of land managers? Here there was clear evidence given by the perpetrator himself of not just the irresponsible exercise of access but the exercise of access knowing that access was being taken over land excluded from the right afforded by the Act. Furthermore when law officers arrived at the request of the land manager they found themselves rightly or wrongly unable to take measures to protect the rights of the land manager because of the claim by the access taker that any dispute was a civil one and not a criminal matter. If there were to be any doubt about the veracity and reliability of the evidence given on behalf of the pursuer that she had concerns for the security of her possessions, her family and herself if access were permitted over the land in question, it was likely to be dispelled by that set of circumstances. It may be that if the person taking access across the lawn had been someone other than Mr M, perhaps wearing a striped jersey and carrying a bag marked 'swag', different action would have been taken by police officers but the land manager cannot be sure. Anyone aware of these circumstances could hardly find themselves in agreement with the evidence of Mr S that the ordinary criminal law could be relied upon to give protection to land managers against persons not exercising access responsibly. If that were the way the Act is put into effect by a person such as the director of the Ramblers Association what can one expect of others whose experience of the code and workings of the Act is much less developed?

CHAPTER SIX

CORE PATHS
AND PATHS

What is a core path? In terms of sections 17 and 18 of the 2003 Act local authorities are obliged to draw up a system of paths ("core paths") sufficient for the purpose of giving the public reasonable access throughout their area.

Section 19 of the 2003 Act gives a local authority power to maintain core paths, keep them free from obstruction and erect signage. Sections 17-19 are referred to for their full terms. The reality is that these core paths have now been created.

Core paths can be reviewed or amended in terms of sections 20, 20A – 20D of the 2003 Act. The matter of reviewing and amending was recently considered in Gartmore House v Loch Lomond & The Trossachs National Park Authority v The Scottish Ministers [2022] CSIH 5 ("Gartmore"). In Gartmore the reclaiming motion (appeal) concerned the respondents' decision to amend the 2010 core path plan for the Loch Lomond & The Trossachs National Park.

For those that lack the time or inclination to read further the appeal was refused. A local authority can review such core path plans unless patently irrational or unreasonable. The mere fact that another authority or reporter might have reached a different decision is immaterial.

The amendments included the addition of two core paths, whereby users could go through land surrounding the petitioners' hotel and accommodation block on the Gartmore Estate. Following a local inquiry, the Scottish Ministers directed the respondents to adopt the amended plan. The petitioners challenge the addition of the paths. The Lord

Ordinary found that both the direction and the adoption were lawful. He refused to reduce these decisions.

The Gartmore case is also noteworthy as it touched upon the Equality Act 2010 section 149:

> *149 Public sector equality duty*
>
> *(1) A public authority must, in the exercise of its functions, have due regard to the need to—*
>
> > *(a) eliminate discrimination, harassment, victimisation and any other conduct that is prohibited by or under* <u>this Act</u> *;*
> >
> > *(b) advance equality of opportunity between persons who share a relevant protected characteristic and persons who do not share it;*
> >
> > *(c) foster good relations between persons who share a relevant protected characteristic and persons who do not share it.*
>
> ...
>
> *The relevant protected characteristics include: age; disability; and religion or belief.*

Gartmore is a charity that owns and operates a hotel and an adjacent accommodation block. The property is used frequently to accommodate groups of children, including vulnerable ones, and by religious groups that require privacy. For example, Green Routes, another charity, provides teaching and support in outdoor activities to persons with learning disabilities.

A core paths plan was first adopted by the respondents in 2010. In 2018, they began a formal consultation to amend the plan by adding further core paths. By letters dated 15 February and 28 October 2019, Gartmore objected to the addition of paths ADD23 and ADD27. The respondents refused to remove them and submitted the objections to the Ministers, who appointed a reporter to carry out a local inquiry (2003 Act, s 18 (4) and s 20A(5)).

Gartmore made representations to the reporter. Their principal concern was that the paths would run through their property, close to the accommodation block and land used by visiting groups. As part of the risk assessment for the activities carried out on the land with children and vulnerable groups, the petitioners required to control access. They would be unable to offer the level of assurance required by local authorities under relevant child protection guidelines. Over half of their users would be affected.

In refusing Gartmore's appeal a decision which flows from a reporter's recommendations in the planning context, the court is seeking only to determine whether that decision is lawful or not.

It will be unlawful only if the decision-maker has: made a material error of law; taken into account an irrelevant consideration; failed to take account of a material consideration; made a critical finding in fact without any basis for doing so; or has reached a decision which no reasonable decision-maker could have reached (*Wordie Property Co v Secretary of State for Scotland 1984 SLT 345*, LP (Emslie) at 347-348). In this case, Gartmore's contentions are primarily based on the first and last considerations.

The 2003 Act imposed an obligation on the respondents to draw up a plan for core paths "sufficient for the purpose of giving the public reasonable access throughout their area" (s 17(1)). The respondents did this.

The adoption of the plan did not carry with it an assumption, or a presumption, that there was thereby a sufficient core paths network in the area; merely that the identified core paths contributed to the statutory purpose of giving reasonable access and balanced the factors, including the interests of land owners, required by section 17(3) . A plan which was put forward for adoption as contributing to the statutory purpose could hardly have been rejected because it did not create a sufficient or saturation level of core paths.

In due course, an adopted plan might be improved; whether by the addition of other paths or the substitution of different routes, provided that the plan, as amended, also contributes to the sufficiency of the network. That is the objective of the provision for review (s 20(1)). The use of the phrase "continues to give... reasonable access" does not carry with it an implication that any previously adopted plan demonstrates the existence of a sufficiency which can never be improved. It would make no practical sense for a core paths plan to be set in aspic.

The reporter asked the correct question of whether, under section 17(1), the new plan with the additional paths created a system which again contributed positively to the overall purpose of giving the public reasonable access; balancing in that equation the land owner's interest. It was not necessary for the reporter to carry out a comparison of the existing network with the proposed new one or to examine whether the network in place was already sufficient. That would be an unduly narrow and artificial exercise; it would run counter to the statutory policy of conferring on authorities a wide discretionary power to review, when they consider it appropriate, whether improvements are desirable in the interests of furthering the objective of promoting reasonable public access.

The review exercise involved a consideration of whether the amended plan continued to provide reasonable access, not whether the existing plan was of itself sufficient. The latter might be an argument which a landowner might advance, and it is no doubt a factor to be considered, but that is all.

The reporter explained the deficiencies in the existing plan, notably that some of the paths were along public roads. They did not give access to the areas surrounding the village, as distinct from the village itself. The new paths would improve access in a number of specific ways, including loops and links. There was no difficulty in understanding the reporter's reasoning to the effect that the new paths enhanced the existing network. The informed reader was left in no real and substantial doubt about the reporter's reasons or the material considerations which were taken into account (*Wordie Property Co v Secretary of State for Scotland* , LP (Emslie) at 348). The appeal, by judicial review, accordingly failed.

Equality Impact Assessment ("EIA")

Prior to the inquiry, an EIA had been carried out by the respondents in order to ascertain whether there were any barriers which prevented those with protected characteristics from participating in the process and presenting their arguments to the reporter. This had resulted in a consideration of the adequacy of the consultation process. The steps taken were duly recorded in the EIA.

It is no doubt correct to state, at a high-level generality, that whatever might have been submitted to the reporter he remained under a duty to have due regard to the various factors specified in section 149 of the Equality Act 2010 .

The court agreed with *Baker v Communities and Local Government Secretary [2009] PTSR 809 (Dyson LJ at para 36)* .

However, the context in which the reporter was operating was a local inquiry for which measures had been taken to ensure equality in participation. The reporter heard submissions about those with a protected characteristic. It was then his function to reach a recommendation based on the submissions made to him by the respondents and the objectors, including the petitioners, rather than engaging in any inquisitorial frolic (*Taylor v Scottish Ministers (No. 2) 2019 SLT 681* , LP (Carloway), delivering the opinion of the court, at paras [34] and [35]).

The reporter addressed the matters which were raised before him in relation to the public sector equality duty. These concerned the interruption, or disruption, of the activities of children, vulnerable persons and religious groups. The reporter reasoned that the limited scope of any interference, and the ability to temper the effects of such interference by taking temporary measures, was not such as justified a refusal to incorporate new paths which would enhance the access rights of all.

The exercise was one of balancing the different weights to be attached to the matters raised and reaching a planning judgement on where the scales came to rest. The reporter reached a view on the relative weights; a matter which is not susceptible to review.

There was no need for the reporter to make a specific reference to the Equality Act 2010 when he had done what was important; addressed the specific problems raised by the petitioners and Green Routes in relation to those with protected characteristics (*Baker v Communities and Local Government Secretary*, Dyson LJ at para 37). Once more, there is no difficulty in understanding the reporter's reasoning and the material considerations which were taken into account. The challenge on this basis also failed.

Path agreements

In terms of section 21 of the 2003 Act a local authority may enter an agreement (a "path agreement") with a person having the necessary power for the delineation and maintenance or, as the case may be, for the delineation, creation and maintenance of a path within land in respect of which access rights are exercisable. A path agreement shall be on such terms and conditions as to payment or otherwise as may be specified in it.

Notwithstanding the preceding paragraph core paths do not require to be constructed or maintained to any particular standard. It may not be obvious when one is actually on a core paths. A pavement or an unmade track through a forest may form parts of a core path. Nevertheless, paths for all (pathsforall.org.uk) contains helpful information on (i) managing paths for wildlife, (ii) general design, (iii) installing signage, and (iv) maintenance. Paths for all also contains suggested health walks including walks that are described as dementia friendly, cancer friendly and buggy friendly. The website has a very helpful postcode or place search function.

Additional Local Authority powers to delineate paths

Where agreement cannot be reached in terms of section 21 of the 2003 Act section 22, to be read in conjunction with schedule 1, gives a local authority compulsory power.

A local authority may make a path order. Any such order made can be revoked. Any such order must contain a map showing the delineation of the path.

In terms of section 2297) of the 2003 Act where access rights have (a) by virtue of any provision of this Part of the 2003 Act, not been exercisable over any land consisting of a public path created under sections 30 to 36 of the Countryside (Scotland) Act 1967 (c. 86); but (b) becomes exercisable over that land, the public path creation agreement or the public path creation order or public path diversion order by which the public path was created shall, for the purposes of the exercise of access rights, be treated as a path agreement or, as the case may be, a path order.

Ploughing etc

Sometimes core paths or rights of way cross fields that are ploughed from time to time. Section 23 permits such ploughing "in accordance with good husbandry." Section 23 only allows this for 14 days beginning on the day on which the path or right of way is disturbed (unless the local authority agrees to a longer period. If the landowner fails to comply that is an offence in terms of section 23 (3). Notwithstanding section 23(3) section 24 gives a local authority remedial powers to reinstate an obstructed path or right of way.

CHAPTER SEVEN

RANGERS AND LOCAL ACCESS FORUMS

In terms of section 24 of the 2003 Act a local authority, at its discretion, may appoint persons to act as rangers in relation to any land in respect of which access rights are exercisable. Rangers have the power to enter any land in respect of which access rights are exercisable. The purposes for which such rangers may be so appointed are:

(a) to advise and assist the owner of the land and other members of the public as to any matter relating to the exercise of access rights in respect of the land; and

(b) to perform such other duties in relation to the exercise of those rights in respect of that land as the local authority determine.

Whilst a local authority **may** appoint rangers it **must**, in terms of section 25 of the Act, establish a local access forum ("LAF"). In terms of section 25(2) of the 2003 Act the functions of the LAF are:

(a) to advise the local authority and any other person or body consulting the forum on matters having to do with the exercise of access rights, the existence and delineation of rights of way or the drawing up and adoption of a plan for a system of core paths under sections 17 and 18 above;

(b) to offer and, where the offer is accepted, to give assistance to the parties to any dispute about—

(i) the exercise of access rights;

(ii) the existence and delineation of rights of way;

> (iii) *the drawing up and adoption of the plan referred to in paragraph (a) above; or*
>
> (iv) *the use of core paths,*
>
> *towards the resolution of the dispute.*

Sections 25 (4) and 25(5) provide that the composition of the board should cover various interests:

> (a) *ensuring reasonable representation in the forum of—*
>
> > (i) *bodies representative of persons with an interest in any of the matters mentioned in subsection (2)(b)(i) to (iv) above;*
> >
> > (ii) *persons having such an interest;*
> >
> > (iii) *bodies representative of the owners of land in respect of which access rights are exercisable or in which there is a core path; and*
> >
> > (iv) *owners of such land, and*
>
> (b) *ensuring a reasonable balance among those mentioned in sub-paragraphs (i) to (iv) of paragraph (a) above.*
>
> (5) *The local authority may appoint one or more of its own members to a local access forum.*

More than one local access forum may be established for the area of a local authority (25 (6)).

The work of LAF is essential to the harmonious operation of the provisions of the 2003 Act. It has been said that existence of such forums, and their representative constitution, has kept litigation to a minimum.

There is a LAF "guide to good practice", (2nd edition) 2006, available in PDF format at www.outdoorsaccess-scotland.scot. As it extends to 80 pages a summary here would be a dis-service

CHAPTER EIGHT

CASE LAW

For those without a legal background it should be understood that there is a hierarchy of courts in Scotland being (i) Sheriff Courts, (ii) the Sheriff Appeal Court-Civil ("SAC"), and (iii) the Court of Session. When an appeal from the SAC is heard in the Court of Session this is before what is known as the "Inner House" ("COS"). It is unusual for the SAC to allow cases of this nature to be further appealed to the COS. The higher the court the more binding its decision is (precedent).

As this is intended to be a practical guide Anstalt v Loch Lomond and Trossachs National Park Authority [2018] CSIH 22 ("Anstalt") is discussed extensively being the most recent and binding authority on the issues discussed in this book; particularly sections 6 and 14 of the 2003 Act. Anstalt disapproves/overrules Tuley v Highland Council [2009] S.C 456 and Aviemore Highland Resort Limited v Cairngorm National Park Authority 2009 S.L.T (Sh Ct) 97. Accordingly, these cases are not extensively discussed so as to avoid confusion as to what the settled law is.

Anstalt

Renyana Stahl Anstalt, landowner, owned an estate in the Trossachs, near Aberfoyle, extending to 1500 hectares. Approximately 120 hectares, containing a farmhouse and outbuildings, at the Drumlean Estate was enclosed by deer fencing with two gates. Some cattle and deer were within the fenced area (wild boar had previously been there).

Wild boar seem to have become popular in Scotland with landowners since the 2003 Act came into force. A "Danger Wild Boar" sign had been erected at the request of the local authority. As an aside, In August 2022 a black panther was apparently spotted near Aberdour with numerous claimed sightings throughout Scotland. It remains to be seen if prides of panthers will replace wild boar.

Anstalt sought to limit and discourage access to a 120 hectare area. Three gates were left locked. The "Danger Wild Boar" sign remained despite the sign outstaying the presence of the boar. The practical effect of the locked gates was to restrict access to 10% of the entire estate.

The relevant authority, the national park authority, issued a section 14 notice insisting that the gates were unlocked and the signage removed. The section 14 notice started a chain of events being:

(1) An Appeal to the Sheriff at Stirling;

(2) An Appeal of the Sheriff's judgment to the SAC and

(3) a further Appeal from the S.A.C to the COS.

Sheriff Court

Anstalt raised a summary application. The Sheriff ruled against the authority and allowed the appeal. The summary application was raised in terms of section 14(4) of the 2003 Act in respect of a notice served by the local authority on the pursuers all in terms of section 14(2) of the 2003 Act.

On 12th February 2016 the sheriff allowed the appeal. He did so as in erecting the signs and locking the gates Anstalt had, subjectively, been acting for a legitimate land management reason. The Sheriff, applying the "subjective" test appears to have followed Tuley (*infra*) and this is where matters started to unravel. If, looked through the eyes of a landowner acting in good faith, there were legitimate reasons for locked gates and signage that would suffice. In reliance on *Aviemore Highland Resort Ltd v Cairngorms National Park Authority 2009 S.L.T. (Sh Ct) 97,*

[2009] 6 WLUK 749, had found that as the gates had been in place, and locked, and the sign erected since before the 2003 Act came into force, the appellants were not owners of land in respect of which access rights were exercisable.

SAC

On 12th February 2016 the local authority appealed to the SAC and on 30th March 2017 the SAC allowed the appeal thereby overturning the Sheriff's decision.

The SAC ordered that the gates be opened and the sign be removed. It did so as, in the court's view, there were not legitimate reasons for the locked gates and signage. The SAC ordered that all 3 gates be opened and the wild boar sign removed.

The Sheriff's obiter dictum in *Tuley (infra)* was to the effect that it was the subjective purpose of the landowner which had to be considered. The SAC observed that although purpose was to be assessed subjectively, whether an owner was acting responsibly was to be assessed objectively, having regard inter alia to the Scottish Outdoor Access Code.

The SAC further determined that while Aviemore Highland Resort had been correctly decided on its facts, the position was different where it concerned a continuing failure to unlock the gates contrary to s.14(1)(e). The farm was land to which the 2003 Act applied and over which access rights were exercisable and as the main purpose had been to deter persons from taking access, the appellants were not entitled to continue to refuse access. Assessing the evidence subjectively, the SAC accordingly rejected the Sheriff's finding on purpose. This again raises an interesting issue as to what extent a higher court and re-assess evidence and make its own findings; McGraddie v McGraddie [2013] UKSC 58.

COS

On 16th May 2017, permission to appeal to the COS was granted. On 27th March 2018 the COS refused the appeal and essentially, with slight differences, upheld the SAC's judgment. The COS ordered that only two of three gates required to be open to afford reasonable access. It did not order the removal of the wild boar sign as Stirling Council had required it in relation to an earlier herd of wild boar.

Was the SAC correct in understanding the ratio of Aviemore Highland Resort? Yes. Unless the land was excepted under s.6, it was land to which the rights attached and it then became the duty of the landowner under s.3 to use and manage it, and otherwise conduct the ownership of it, in a way in which was responsible as respected those rights.

Where there was a right to cross and be on the farm area, the only responsible action was to permit the rights to be exercised by allowing access which had to involve unlocking any gates and removing any signs which prevented or deterred such access; paragraph 59.

The land in question was land over which access rights under the 2003 Act were exercisable and the respondents were, as a generality, entitled to take action in respect of those rights under sections 14(1) of the 2003 Act; paragraph 61.

Were the sheriff and SAC correct to follow the obiter dictum in Tuley? No. Section 14 did not refer to the landowners' purpose as such but to the landowners' acts which were what had to be looked at objectively to see what their main purpose was and the court had to decide, looking objectively at all the circumstances, what the main purpose of locking the gates and putting up the notice was; paragraph 64. The sheriff and SAC were in error in proceeding on the basis that the issue of purpose fell to be resolved by a determination of the honesty, bona fides or credibility of the pursuers' agent and the fundamental problem with their approach, which had understandably been formed in the light of the obiter dictum in Tuley, was that it regarded such issues as, in effect, determinative; paragraph 66.

When the merits were reconsidered, the inevitable conclusion was that the main purpose of locking the gates was to deter persons from exercising their rights of access and transit under section 1 of the 2003 Act.

The Inner House commented that the testimony led before the sheriff had little bearing on the central issue to be determined and while some evidence about land management might be useful, the arguments in relation to the propensities of cattle and deer were unsustainable in the context of 120 hectares and the presence of cattle and deer could not objectively be a reasonable reason for preventing the public from accessing the area. Responsible land management could accommodate public access by the creation of paths and the use of signage, effectively encouraging access to defined parts of the land; paragraph 67-69.

One crumb of comfort to Anstalt was that the appeal from the S.A.C failed on the central issues in dispute but failing to unlock the main gate would not contravene section 14 (1) once the other gates were unlocked since it would not then be deterring or preventing access, and erecting the wild boar sign on the main gate did not contravene s.14(1) when it was done at the local authority's request; paragraphs 73-79. This raises the issue as to whether landowners can accumulate warning signs before re-homing wild boars and panthers etc.

The Inner House also held that a remit of the cause to the sheriff would have been highly unusual in the circumstances where the power to do so should not be used to allow a reconsideration of the merits of a cause by a judge or sheriff who had already decided them. The sheriff has obviously formed a view and it is suggested that the Inner House were indeed correct in disapproving a remit to "consider of new".

Human Rights

Anstalt also touched upon a human rights challenge. The Inner House held that Anstalt's right to a fair and public hearing in terms of the ECHR art.6 had been adequately protected where they had been able to challenge the defenders' notice by making a summary application to the sheriff; paragraph 76. The other challenge regarding any retrospective effect of the 2003 Act did not arise where the gates had been both replaced and frequently unlocked since the 2003 Act was introduced but even had they been permanently locked, the enforcement of remedial requirements under section 14(1)(e) of the 2003 Act did not involve any retrospective effect. Even assuming the 2003 Act created new rights as distinct from re-enacting those thought by some to arise at common law, they were rights which had a prospective nature; paragraph 78.

In the opinion of the court the right to be on, or to cross, the pursuers' estate was entirely without prejudice to their right as landowners to erect such fences or walls in the vicinity of the farmhouse and other buildings sufficient to protect their privacy and safety of persons living and working there, and the security of items kept there, and if there were a dispute about what expanse of land that might cover. The pursuers could, as others have, seek a declarator under s.28 of the 2003 Act seeking to exclude specific areas from those over which access could be taken; paragraph 57.

Pre-Anstalt the undernoted cases illustrate the issues that arose in interpreting the 2003 Act; particularly section 6 . These cases turn on their own facts, circumstances and the geographical features of the properties in question.

Gloag v Perth and Kinross Council and the Ramblers' Association 2007 S.C.L.R 530 was the first reported cases on the issues arising from sections 1 and 6. The case is worth reading as it also deals with section 7 (5) of the 2003 Ac that provides:

'7.5 There are included among the factors which go to determine what extent of land is sufficient for the purposes mentioned in section 6(1)(b)(vi) above, the location and other characteristics of the house or other place.'

The case also makes interesting reading for its commentary on the Section 10 of the Act that also deals the after mentioned Scottish Outdoor Access Code:

"**10.** *The Scottish Outdoor Access Code*

    (1) It is the duty of Scottish Natural Heritage to draw up and issue a code, to be known as the Scottish Outdoor Access Code, setting out, in relation to access rights, guidance as to the circumstances in which—

        (a) those exercising these rights are to be regarded as doing so in a way which is or is not responsible;

        (b) persons are to be regarded as carrying on activities, otherwise than in the course of exercising access rights, in a way which is likely to affect the exercise of these rights by other persons;

        (c) owners of land in respect of which these rights are exercisable
        are to be regarded as using and managing, or otherwise conducting the ownership of it, in a way which is or is not responsible;

        (d) owners of land in respect of which these rights are not exercisable are to be regarded as using and managing, or otherwise conducting the ownership of it, in a way which is likely to affect the exercise of these rights on land which is contiguous to that land.'

The proceedings were brought by summary application in terms of section 28 of the 2003 Act. Section 28 and how to litigate in such matters is discussed in greater detail later in this book.

Dame Ann Gloag is a businesswoman, activist and charity campaigner. In 2007 the pursuer had a high public profile. The pursuer, a native of Perth, bought a large country house (Kinfauns Castle) near Perth. It has extensive grounds. The dwellinghouse was the family home for the pursuer, her husband and family members. The pursuer and defenders could not agree on what might be a reasonable area of ground in and around the house to afford her reasonable privacy and security (theft and possible kidnap).

For the pursuer it was argued that the high profile nature of the pursuer required a larger area of ground to be sufficient to enable her to have privacy because of press interest in her activities and because of possible criminal interest in her and her family because of the wide knowledge of her business success and earnings. She collected paintings which had a substantial value and there was a likelihood that attempts might be made to break into the premises. Her human rights would be breached if a sufficient area of ground was not allowed.

The local authority argued that the amount of land chosen by the pursuer was excessive and proposed a smaller area. They argued that it was not appropriate to fix the amount of ground by virtue of the desires of the owner of the property for the time being. The security concerns of the pursuer were not relevant because the size of the ground should not change according to the desires of the individual owner for the time being. The code should be used as an aid to come to a decision on what land is sufficient.

The second defenders (Ramblers) argued that the legislation created a generalised, wide-ranging series of mutual rights and obligations in relation to access to and over land however it was held and used, from which departure should be sanctioned only in compelling and carefully prescribed circumstances and this case did not demonstrate such circumstances. The approach of the 2003 Act was reciprocal, or mutual and any decision as to whether or not land was to be excluded from access had to take into account the rights of the access taker as well as the rights of the landowner.

The second defenders also argued that the owner of a house could not take advantage of the exception unless he could demonstrate that the exception was necessary for the enjoyment of the house and that the question came to be, was the exclusion of any person to the limit of the fence as it stood necessary for the enjoyment of the house? The case for the pursuer was periled on her individual self-interest including security and privacy and if security and other such a similar considerations were placed on one side there was no need for any land in excess of the area suggested by the respondents.

In finding for the pursuer the court held:

(1)   that it could not be said that the advice and guidance given by the Scottish Outdoor Access code was a direct help to the interpretation of s 6 of the Act and any suggestion that the nature of the ground itself should be decisive as to whether the land should be excluded from the rights of access was misconceived (para [36]);

(2)   that in interpreting s 6 of the Act the courts would have in mind what a reasonable person living in a property of the type under consideration would require to have reasonable measures of privacy and to ensure their enjoyment of that house was not unreasonably disturbed (para [45]); and

(3)   that taking into account security aspects relating to the average owner of the house, the fact that the boundary of the area of ground followed a previously erected fence, the use to which the adjacent ground was put and the relative size of the area of ground applied for exemption, declarator should be granted in terms sought by the pursuer (para [60]); and declarator granted.

Snowie v Stirling Council 2008 S.L.T (Sh Ct 61) ("Snowie") can be contrasted with Gloag. In Snowie the pursuers were only partially successful. The pursuers raised proceedings seeking to exclude a substantial part of their estate, near Kippen, from public access. The action was raised after Stirling Council ("defenders") had served a written notice alleging a contravention of section 23 of the 2003 Act following the pursuers' decision to lock a pedestrian gate. The pursuers sought reasonable privacy and security for themselves and their tenants, submitting that this standard was to be measured by the standards of the persons affected in the house in which the privacy was sought, and contended that they had never seen any genuine ramblers.

The pursuers' application was granted in part. Foreshadowing Anstalt the test of reasonableness was objective, and in interpreting section 6 the court was obliged to determine what a reasonable person living in a property of the type under consideration would require to have to enjoy reasonable measures of privacy and to ensure enjoyment of the house was not unreasonably disturbed.

It was clear that the security of the estate would not be compromised by the opening of the pedestrian gate when considering the public right of way and two public roads adjacent to the estate together with the number of tenants and access taken in relation to stables. It was reasonable to protect an area extending to a substantial portion to the front of the pursuers' property, and the whole of the rear garden, as truly private.

The notion the tenants would suffer was unsustainable where each had a well-defined garden area, and no reasonable access taker could misunderstand the ground attaching to each of the tenanted properties.

The court observed, foreshadowing Anstalt, that a subjective test would lead to the possibility of repeated applications being made depending on the particular views, concerns, family circumstances and even prejudices of a particular proprietor, which could not be the purpose of the 2003 Act. With reference to the Gloag case can that not also be said in relation to security concerns?

Creelman v Argyll & Bute Council 2009 S.L.T (Sh Ct) 165 ("Creelman") concerned a property in rural Argyllshire. The Creelmans' property consisted of a dwellinghouse and other buildings, sat in about 6.5 acres. It adjoined another property (a castle) with these two properties having been joined by an access track.

The pursuers appealed by summary application against a notice issued by the local authority ("defender") under section 14(2) of the 2003 Act. The notice required the removal of a sign erected at the entrance to a track stating that access was forbidden without permission. The pursuers also sought declarator under section 28 of the 2003 Act that access rights were not exercisable over their land.

The court determined that rural land, upon which two properties were joined by an access track, was land over which access rights were not exercisable, pursuant to the 2003 Act section 6 (1) (b) (iv). This was because the area of ground was relatively small in respect of the properties and the type of locality, and the track was in close proximity to said properties.

The court allowed the pursuers' appeal and declarator was granted. Access rights were not exercisable over any of the pursuer's land, taking into account s.6(1)(b)(iv) and s.7(5) of the 2003 Act: the area of ground was relatively small in respect of the properties and the type of locality; the track was in close proximity to those properties; and access rights to any part of the adjacent land would affect C's reasonable privacy within what might be said to be their reasonable garden area, which an objective owner would be likely to value to some extent.

The defenders submitted that while access rights ought not to be exercisable over a particular area of the pursuers' land, that land comprised sufficient adjacent land to enable the pursuers to have reasonable measures of privacy whilst allowing members of the public to access the track, and the whole of the pursuer's land was not land over which access rights were not exercisable under s.6(1)(b)(iv) of the 2003 Act.

Where the impetus in this case had not come from disaffected ramblers, the court would not have been persuaded that there was a demand for roaming rights over the ground or that the loss of those rights could be said to be particularly prejudicial;

> *"[12] This dispute had started as a result of the pursuers refusing the owner of the neighbouring property at Dunans Castle permission to use their land for a commercial venture. It seemed that Mr Dickson Spain, the owner thereof, wanted to take visitors to his castle through the pursuers' land as part of a tour. When the pursuers intimated they were not agreeable to this, Mr Dickson Spain had stated, "[T]here is always land reform". Mr Creelman believed that Mr Dickson Spain had made a complaint to the defenders who had then carried certain investigations and gone ahead with the service of the notices."*

Manson v Midlothian Council 2019 S.C.L.R 723 ("Manson") concerned a Landowners' appeal against a notice issued by a local authority under section 14(2) of the 2003 Act requiring the removal of a fence, gate and signs to permit access would be refused where the land in question was land over which access rights under the 2003 Act were exercisable. The sheriff, correctly, determined that the landowners' acts had to be looked at objectively to see what their main purpose that, in the present case, was to deter persons from exercising their rights of access under s.1 of the 2003 Act.

The circumstances were that proprietors of semi-rural land, which was bounded by an unpaved track which led to an adjacent housing estate, appealed by summary application under section 14 (4) of the 2003 Act against a notice issued by a local authority under s.14(2) of the 2003 Act. The notice required the removal of a fence, gate and signs erected on the track, and further sought declarator under s.28 that access rights were not exercisable over the land.

The property was on a private road which served six other residential properties, and the road formed into the path. A vehicular right of access existed over the path and the road in favour of the proprietors of the adjacent estate and an old gate which was on the path had been opened to facilitate access.

The path was situated adjacent to a woodland area being approximately 20 metres from the proprietors' house. It had been used by the neighbouring proprietors and members of the public to access the housing estate prior to the erection of the fence and gate on 4 June 2016.

The applicants averred that they had been aware of some anti-social behaviour on the path prior to their purchase of the land and construction of the property in 2012 but claimed that the level of anti-social behaviour had significantly increased, however, evidence was led from the police that since 2012, there had been no significant increase in the reports of anti-social behaviour on the path, which was supported by the evidence of council employees and proprietors of nearby properties that there had not been any significant anti-social behaviour in the area.

The applicants maintained that the fence and gate had not contravened s.14(1) where their primary purpose in erecting it had been to prevent or deter access along the path by persons who had hitherto exercised their rights of access in an irresponsible manner and it had remained locked due to the irresponsible access and antisocial behaviour, and that the notice was contrary to their rights under ECHR art.8 and ECHR Protocol 1 article 1. They sought declarator on the basis of s.6(1)(b)(iv) of the 2003 Act.

The Application was dismissed.

Was the land excluded under s.28? No. On a strict reading of s.6(1)(b)(iv), the path could not truly be said to be "adjacent" land for the purposes of s.6 and therefore could not fulfil the requirements of that section. In the result, in all the circumstances, viewed objectively using the standard of a reasonable person, the rest of the property, excluding the path, allowed sufficient adjacent land for the purposes of s.6(1)(b)(iv) and, therefore, the path did not fall within that land.

Had the fence and gate contravened s.14(1)? Yes. The applicants' acts made it clear that the purpose of erecting the fence and gate had been to prevent or deter persons from exercising their rights of access under s.1: they had been aware of the use of the path, had not warned or contacted the defender in advance to give notice of their intention to block it and had not attempted to facilitate access by responsible access takers. The path was land over which access rights under the 2003 Act were exercisable and there was no basis for recall of the s.14 notice where the defender was entitled to take action as respects those rights under s.14(1) and the applicants' argument to the contrary fell to be rejected.

Had the s.14 notice contravened the applicants' Convention rights? No. The 2003 Act was not said to be incompatible with the applicants' Convention rights and the wording of the 2003 Act which set out the balanced framework of rights, duties and obligations on all parties involved in the exercise of access rights was itself designed to be Convention-compliant. In any event, the admissibility restriction in art.35 did not apply unless the jurisdiction of the ECHR was sought to be invoked. Further, the evidence demonstrated that there had been engagement with the human rights issues by the council officers, that the decision to serve the s.14 notice had not been pre-determined and that it had been correctly made in terms of the provisions of the 2003 Act, and the applicants' Convention rights had been properly taken into account. The notice had not contravened the applicants' Convention rights.

CHAPTER NINE

ANIMALS

Although the Code addresses the safety and wellbeing of animals (e.g. don't let dogs worry sheep) this is a serious issue that merits further attention. It is understandable that landowners (specifically farmers) grow very weary of dogs that are not kept under proper control.

Readers should be aware of the Dogs (Protection of Livestock) (Amendment) (Scotland) Act 2021 that has sought to address this real problem. The 2021 Act is referred to for its full terms but seeks to reinforce criminal sanctions against irresponsible dog owners by amending The Dogs (Protection of Livestock) Act 1953. Worrying or attacking can lead to 12 months imprisonment, a £40,000 fine (or both). It is important that dog owners realise that the mere presence of a dog near, say, a flock of sheep can cause distress. The 2021 has obvious statutory exceptions such as sheep dogs doing what they are supposed to do.

In relation to landowners and visitors they should also be aware of the Animals (Scotland) Act 1987. The 1987 Act is referred to for its full terms but brings in, in certain circumstances, for any injury or damage caused by certain animals. Section 1 (5) of the 1987 Act provides that there will be no liability has been caused by the mere presence of animal on a road or in any other place.

What if a visitor is cornered by an angry bull or wild boar? Section 4 of the 1987 Act entitles the visitor to injure or kill the animal if self-defence, self-defence of another or self defence of other livestock can be proved. Any such self-defence must be reported to the police within 24 hours. Self-defence is defined in section 4(4) of the 1987 Act. Readers are discouraged from becoming amateur matadors.

The 1987 Act hasn't generated a lot of case law. In <u>Foskett v McClymont</u> <u>1998 S.L.T 892</u> the pursuer sought damages for personal injury when injured by a bull. The court held that the 1987 Act abolished the previous distinction between animals *ferae naturae* and *mansuetae naturae*, with reference to the pre 1987 Act common law was of no assistance in considering the point at issue. Bulls could form a "species" in terms of section 1 (1) (b) of the 1987 Act. The pursuer was accordingly entitled to lead evidence that bulls as a species were likely to cause injury.

CHAPTER TEN

OCCUPIERS' LIABILITY

Occupier's Liability is a practical concern. Landowners and visitors should be aware of sections 1 and 2 of the concise Occupiers' Liability (Scotland) Act 1960 ("1960 Act) being as follows:

Variation of rules of common law as to duty of care owed by occupiers

(1) *The provisions of the next following section of this Act shall have effect, in place of the rules of the common law, for the purpose of determining the care which a person occupying or having control of land or other premises (in this Act referred to as an " occupier of premises ") is required, by reason of such occupation or control, to show towards persons entering on the premises in respect of dangers which are due to the state of the premises or to anything done Or omitted to be done on them and for which he is in law responsible.*

(2) *Nothing in those provisions shall be taken to alter the rules of the common law which determine the person on whom in relation to any premises a duty to show care as aforesaid towards persons entering thereon is incumbent.*

(3) *Those provisions shall apply, in like manner and to the same extent as they do in relation to an occupier of premises and to persons entering thereon.—*

    (a) *in relation to a person occupying or having control of any fixed or moveable structure, including any vessel, vehicle or aircraft, and to persons entering thereon; and*

(b) *in relation to an occupier of premises or a person occupying or having control of any such structure and to property thereon, including the property of persons who have not themselves entered on the premises or structure.*

2 Extent of occupier's duty to show care

(1) *The care which an occupier of premises is required, by reason of his occupation or control of the premises, to show towards a person -entering thereon in respect of dangers which are due to the state of the premises or to anything done or omitted to be done on them and for which the occupier is in law responsible shall, except in so far as he is entitled to and does extend, restrict, modify or exclude by agreement his obligations towards that person, be such care as in all the circumstances of the case is reasonable to see that that person will not suffer injury or damage by reason of any such danger.*

(2) *Nothing in the foregoing subsection shall relieve an occupier of premises of any duty to show in any particular case any higher standard of care which in that case is incumbent on him by virtue of any enactment or rule of law imposing special standards of care on particular classes of persons.*

(3) *Nothing in the foregoing provisions of this Act shall be held to impose on an occupier any obligation to a person entering on his premises in respect of risks which that person has willingly accepted as his; and any question whether a risk was so accepted shall be decided on the same principles as in other cases in which one person owes to another a duty to show care.*

For the avoidance of doubt whilst there is extensive reference to "premises" in the context of 1960 Act this includes "land".

A landowner or occupier does have potential liability in respect of ramblers and visitors to land. They do not enter entirely at their own risk but must take reasonable care for their own safety. Any signage that they do enter at their own risk is of no legal validity; a landowner or occupier can't "contract out" of the 1960 or 2003 Acts.

Sections 5 (2) of the 2003 Act, subject to section 22(4), provides that the extent of the duty of care owed by an occupier of land to another person present on the land is not affected by this Part of the Act or by its operation.

Section 22(4) relates to when a local authority has control of a path in terms of a section 22 "path order". Regard may be had, in determining whether a local authority has control of a path for the purposes of the Occupiers' Liability (Scotland) Act 1960 (c. 30), to the duties imposed by subsection (3) above. The Scottish Outdoor Access Code also imposes duties.

In the context of the foregoing what can be reasonably expected of the landowner/occupier?

The law remains that that an occupier of land containing natural phenomena which presented obvious dangers is not required to take precautions against persons becoming injured by reason of those dangers unless there are special risks such as unusual or unseen sources of danger.

There is no requirement to fence off, or erect warning signs, rivers or cliffs. However, if a steep drop or cliff isn't readily visible, such as a cliff or old mine shaft, it is arguable that fences and warning signs are required. In assessing risk and assessing what is reasonable a question can be posed and answered. Could a rambler inadvertently sustain injury due to a natural hazard that isn't obvious? If so, reasonable steps should be taken to fence off such a hazard or at least erect warning signs.

Landowners and occupiers may derive general guidance of what is expected of them with reference to the following recent cases. These recent cases illustrate whether, albeit again with the "facts and circumstances" *caveat*, where liability may arise.

In Fegan v Highland Council [2007] CSIH 44 the pursuer sought damages in respect of injuries sustained after she fell off a cliff. In finding the defender not liable the court held that there was no obligation to erect a fence or warning signs where a cliff was an obvious hazard. The law remained as stated historically to the general effect that an occupier of land containing natural phenomena which presented obvious dangers was not required to take precautions against persons becoming injured by reason of those dangers unless there were special risks such as unusual or unseen sources of danger; and the location of the seat in the present case did not amount to such.

In Cowan v Hopetoun House Preservation Trust, [2013] CSOH9 the pursuer sued for injuries where, in the dark, he fell into a "ha-ha" (a feature consisting of a turfed ditch, one side of which was sloping and the other vertical and faced with stone or brick) in the grounds of a stately home. The pursuer chose a short cut across the lawn and fell into the ha-ha thereby breaking his ankle.

Did the ha-ha, in darkness, constitute a natural and obvious dangers in respect of which there was a duty of care on the occupiers? The court found the defender liable (albeit with a finding of 75% contributory negligence). The ha-ha, while a permanent and long established feature of Hopetoun's landscape, was an unusual feature, and bringing members of the public onto Hopetoun's grounds in the dark was a relatively unusual event, and the ha ha constituted a danger due to the state of the premises.

In McKevitt v National Trust for Scotland 2018 Rep. L.R 76 a visitor sued for injuries sustained when she fell in the garden ground. A stone on the left side of a path was concealed by lichen causing her to fall. In finding the occupier not liable, the court held that in order to be categorised as an obvious danger, the feature had to be physically obvious and it had to be obvious that it presented a danger. The risk of harm was not foreseeable and the stone only became more difficult to see if a number of conditions existed including the presence of vegetation and certain lighting, and if a person was standing so close to it that the main aspect was the top surface. The standard of reasonable care did not require that steps be taken to guard against something which was a remote possibility.

Notwithstanding a general exception, section 6(i) (e) (ii) of the 2003 Act, golf courses are potentially dangerous places. There is an obvious risk of golfers or, in the context of this book, ramblers or visitors being injured by stray golf balls. The recent case of Phee v Gordon [2013] CSIH 13 gives some assistance on how golf clubs should approach potential liability in terms of the 1960 Act.

At paragraph 23 of the judgment the court noted that there have been several reported cases in golf clubs have been sued when a player has been injured by a ball struck by another golfer. The court stressed that decisions on liability for common law negligence in relation to golfing accidents are very fact specific. It is dangerous to lift *dicta* from one case and apply them in another.

Notwithstanding the foregoing fact specific *caveat* the court confirmed that it was foreseeable that the conflict between players at the *locus* posed a foreseeable danger. It is arguable and logical that ramblers exercising their right to roam (albeit restricted by section 9(f) of the 2003 Act-golf courses excluded) (although sticking to any designated paths, would also be at similar risk.

In these circumstances warning notices should have been erected given the risk of wayward golf balls. Would it not also be reasonable and practicable to erect netting at parts of the course where wayward balls were likely to hit those walking on paths?

CHAPTER ELEVEN

DISPUTE RESOLUTION

There are ways to resolve a dispute under the 2003 Act without resorting to a section 28 Summary Application determination. This obviously depends on the goodwill and common sense of all parties to the dispute.

Involving the LAF would be a good starting point. There can be discussion between interested parties to try and agree a compromise. It is sometimes said that a good outcome in such circumstances is one which none of the parties is totally happy with.

How might such a compromise work in practice? A landowner might seek a section 6 exclusion of 12 acres of ground around a house. A compromise might be effected where, by agreement, any restriction might be restricted to 8 acres and over a different area. The privacy or security concerns might not apply to the entire perimeter of the 12-acre area.

Mediation can be explored although this is not without cost. What is mediation? It is a flexible process that may be used to resolve disputes arising under the 2003 Act. An independent mediator helps parties focus on what the issues are. The mediator is impartial, independent and leaves parties in control of the ultimate outcome. The mediation is confidential. If parties can't agree a section 28 summary application to the court is still open to them. The Scottish Mediation Helpline (0131 556 8118) (admin@scottishmediation.org.uk) can assist further.

As commented earlier if the LAF is not actively a party to any dispute, and not "taking a position", its input could greatly assist in any negotiations or in a quasi mediation function short of an actual mediation. It is part of the function of an LAF to encourage dialogue and to try and resolve disputes

The advantages of a negotiated resolution go beyond a saving in costs. It is often the case that disputes under the 2003 Act have similarities to neighbour disputes and, furthermore, become politicised. As time passes positions become more entrenched. With a negotiated settlement common sense is a winner. Litigated actions leave a "victor" and "vanquished" often in close proximity to each other.

Notwithstanding the foregoing as a last resort a court must determine the disputed issues.

CHAPTER TWELVE

COURT-SUMMARY APPLICATION

It is recommended that wherever possible, any work such as legal drafting, be undertaken by a Solicitor, Solicitor Advocate or Advocate. The following matters should be considered.

Expenses/Affordability

A local authority may have different concerns. It has statutory enforcement duties and must respond to proceedings brought against it.

In the case of private owners, be they land owners or ramblers, litigating in such matters is expensive; particularly if Counsel is instructed. The main methods of funding are (i) private, (ii) legal aid, (iii) crowd funding and legal expenses insurance. Those that use assistive technology can also obtain details in an accessible format; info@pathsforall.org.uk.

There are no provisions for Protective Expenses Orders in the Sheriff Court for this type of action. "How will I fund this?" is therefore an important question for most.

Productions

In preparing such an action for court it will hopefully be the case that most of the preparation has been undertaking in attempting to resolve matters extra-judicially. Before any action is commenced what productions are required to successfully pursue or defend it? The following are the likely productions required in a typical action:

1. Titles and legible title plans (actual titles or evidential extracts).

2. Larger scale OS maps if available.

3. Photographs of signs, paths, gates and any features under discussion (including grid references for these) or signs /features being the subject of Notices.

4. Drone footage. On the assumption that a Sheriff may be unwilling or unable to visit the property drone footage can greatly assist understanding matters. In 2023 drones are used for a variety of peaceful purposes.

5. Copies of Notices issued including those forming the subject matter of the action

6. Expert's report?

Site visit

On the motion of parties a Sheriff may visit the subjects.

Titles

Unless copy titles have been agreed or admitted the actual titles should be lodged. Are the titles actually legible? If not, can they be transcribed for easier reading?

OS Maps

These can be found at osmaps.com. Such maps will show the topography of land that may not be so clear on a title plan. They may also show public rights of way and core paths. Older OS maps may also show the historic existence of paths and features.

Photographs

In most cases photographs of disputed signs or gates will be the best evidence practically available. Can the details of what any photograph depicts be agreed in a Joint Minute of Admissions (essentially a contract between parties that agrees undisputed evidence)? Can the GPS co-ordinates of any such features also be agreed?

Drone footage

Even prior to world events in 2022 drones were being used more extensively. Parties should attempt to agree, in a Joint Minute, what any drone footage depicts; e.g. "This shows the main drive from the Notice at its entrance marked "A", on the plan to the Notice at the Steading marked "B" on the plan.

Expert's report

Is an expert required (paragraph 69 of Anstalt is food for thought)? The traits of certain animals are apparently within judicial knowledge. In some of the above reported cases experts gave evidence with reliance on their evidence, particularly on security issues, varying from case to case. Any expert should be chosen with great care. It is not enough for an expert to have "expertise". The expert must come across well; as an impartial expert and not a "hired gun".

In Gloag security experts gave evidence with their evidence apparently assisting the court:

> "[8] I was satisfied from the evidence given by the experts, which I accepted, that a person having the profile that Mrs Gloag has would require higher than usual security, partly because of heightened press interest in her activities and partly because of possible heightened criminal interest in her family and possessions.

The evidence did not show on a balance of probabilities that such an immediate risk to her personal security did in fact exist but it did demonstrate in my opinion that it was not unreasonable for the pursuer in this case to take precautions against the possibility of such risks and to be mindful of the possibility of criminal activities against her or her property."

In Snowie the learned Sheriff assessed some of the expert evidence as less persuasive:

"[36] When he was being cross examined, perfectly properly and fairly, about this omission he dissembled before trying to suggest that the defender's counsel was "sniggering and shaking his head" (at 3/71F), a comment both unwarranted and unworthy. At the very least Mr H showed a sensitivity which would not accord with his years' experience in the police force. At most, he was involved in a strategy which tried to avoid answering questions which he felt might be unhelpful to the pursuer.

[37] I considered whether all of these criticisms could be explained by his lack of experience, but the impression of favouring the Snowies is fortified by the fact that each of his acts and omissions had the effect of bolstering the Snowies' position. If these were a catalogue of naïve and careless errors made by an inexperienced security consultant, one might expect that some resulted in a worsening of the Snowies' position but, from mis-remembering the date of the burglary suffered by the Rosses to the anecdotal evidence of the chief constable's "true" crime figures, to the omission of the right of way (but inclusion of the fertiliser risk and the risk of strangles being introduced), the whole of his evidence was given in a way that demonstrated a commitment to giving evidence entirely favourable to the pursuers, whatever the factual position. I find the evidence of the perceived security threat to be wholly unreliable.

[38] I dwell on Mr H's evidence for two reasons; in the first place it is clear from the Gloag judgment (Ann Gloag v Perth and

Kinross Council , Sheriff Michael Fletcher, Perth sheriff court, 12 June 2007, unreported) that the independent security evidence was material in relation to the ultimate decision in so far as it related to the property, the type of person likely to own such a property and the risks to security and privacy which such persons might face; in the second place Mr H was, on one view, the only wholly independent witness from whom the court heard. (Mr M, whilst having no direct connection with this case can hardly be described as disinterested.) However he failed to approach the matter with the objectivity which the court is entitled to expect from a purportedly independent expert.

[39] The report was clearly prepared with view to the litigation, and Mr H was determined that both the report and he would be entirely supportive of Mr Snowie…"

What is an "expert" in this context? The UK Supreme Court decision of Kennedy v Cordia Services (Scotland) LLP 2016 UKSC 6 gives detailed guidance. Readers are referred to this case for its full terms. The court gave guidance on the use of expert evidence in civil cases, the admissibility of such evidence, the responsibility of a party's legal team to make sure that the expert performed his role, the court's role in policing the performance of the expert's duties, and the consideration of economy in litigation (paras 38-61):

"39. Skilled witnesses, unlike other witnesses, can give evidence of their opinions to assist the court. This gives rise to threshold questions of the admissibility of expert evidence. An example of opinion evidence is whether Miss Kennedy would have been less likely to fall if she had been wearing anti-slip attachments on her footwear."

40. Experts can and often do give evidence of fact as well as opinion evidence. A skilled witness, like any non-expert witness, can give evidence of what he or she has observed if it is relevant to a fact in issue. An example of such evidence in this case is Mr Greasly's evidence of the slope of the pavement on which Miss Kennedy lost her footing. There are no special rules governing the admissibility of such factual evidence from a skilled witness.".....

"52. The Scottish courts have adopted the guidance of Cresswell J on an expert's duties in The Ikarian Reefer [1993] 2 Lloyd's Rep 68 in both civil and criminal matters: see Lord Caplan in Elf Caledonia Ltd v London Bridge Engineering Ltd September 2, 1997 (unreported) at pp 225–227 and Wilson v Her Majesty's Advocate (above) at paras 59 and 60. We quote Cresswell J's summary (at pp 81–82) omitting only case citations:

"The duties and responsibilities of expert witnesses in civil cases include the following:

1. *Expert evidence presented to the court should be, and should be seen to be, the independent product of the expert uninfluenced as to form or content by the exigencies of litigation.*

2. *An expert witness should provide independent assistance to the court by way of objective unbiased opinion in relation to matters within his expertise. An expert witness in the High Court should never assume the role of an advocate.*

3. *An expert witness should state the facts or assumption on which his opinion is based. He should not omit to consider material facts which could detract from his concluded opinion.*

4. *An expert witness should make it clear when a particular question or issue falls outside his expertise.*

5. *If an expert's opinion is not properly researched because he considers that insufficient data is available, then this must be stated with an indication that the opinion is no more than a provisional one. In cases where an expert witness who has prepared a report could not assert that the report contained the*

truth, the whole truth and nothing but the truth without some qualification, that qualification should be stated in the report.

6. *If, after exchange of reports, an expert witness changes his view on a material matter having read the other side's expert's report or for any other reason, such change of view should be communicated (through legal representatives) to the other side without delay and when appropriate to the court.*

7. *Where expert evidence refers to photographs, plans, calculations, analyses, measurements, survey reports or other similar documents, these must be provided to the opposite party at the same time as the exchange of reports."*

Summary Application

What is a Summary Application? A Summary Application, a type of writ or summons initiating a court action, is raised using a Form 1 (Initial Writ) and following the Act of Sederunt (Summary, Applications, Statutory Applications and Appeals Etc. Rules) 1999; see Scottish Courts website. Importantly, it should be printed on reasonable quality, unfolded, A4 paper. Those that require a more detailed discussion on Summary Application procedure are referred to Chapter 26 of MacPhail's Sheriff Court Practice, 4th edition being the generally recognised textbook on the subject.

The Style in Appendix One is just that. It can be adopted, adapted or ignored. Green's litigation Styles and Bennett's Style Writs for the Sheriff Court (Fourth Edition) are other useful sources.

Section 28 of the 2003 Act is the relevant section and provides:

"(1) It is competent, on summary application made to the sheriff, for the sheriff—

(a) *to declare that the land specified in the application is or, as the case may be, is not land in respect of which access rights are exercisable;*

(b) *to declare—*

    (i) *whether a person who has exercised or purported to exercise access rights has exercised those rights responsibly for the purposes of section 2 above;*

    (ii) *whether the owner of land in respect of which access rights are exercisable is using, managing or conducting the ownership of the land in a way which is, for the purposes of section 3 above, responsible.*

(2) *It is competent, on summary application made to the sheriff, for the sheriff to declare whether a path, bridleway or other means of crossing land specified in the application is, or is not, a right of way by foot, horseback, pedal cycle or any combination of those.*

(3) *The proceedings for a declaration under subsection (1) or (2) above are those for an action of declarator initiated by summary application to the sheriff.*

(4) *A summary application for a declaration shall be served on the local authority.*

(5) *The local authority are entitled to be a party to proceedings for a declaration.*

(6) *Where the person seeking a declaration is the owner of the land, it is not necessary to serve the application on any person but the local authority unless subsection (7A) applies].*

(7) *In any other case, the person seeking the declaration shall serve the application on the owner of the land.*

7(A). Where a declaration is being sought under subsection (1)(b)(i), the person seeking the declaration must also serve the application on the person whose exercise or purported exercise of access rights is in question.]

(8) *Rules of court shall provide—*

(a) *for the circumstances in which (including any time periods within which) a summary application may be made for the purposes of this section;*

(b) *for public notice of the making of summary applications for the purposes of this section;*

(c) *for enabling persons interested in the exercise of access rights over specific land or, as the case may be, in the existence of a right of way over specific land and persons or bodies representative of such persons to be parties to the proceedings;*

(d) *for limiting the number of persons and bodies who may be such parties.*

(9) *This section is without prejudice to any remedy otherwise available in respect of rights conferred and duties imposed by or under this Part of this Act.*

In addition to section 28 anyone contemplating such proceedings should be familiar with the Summary Application Rules; Act of Sederunt (Summary Applications, Statutory Applications and Appeals Etc. Rules) 1999. The rules are referred to for their full terms. They are available on line and, note for practitioners, in volume 2 of Greens Sheriff Court and Sheriff Appeal Court Rules (2021-2022 at time of writing).

Rule, 2.2 A, provides for lay support in certain circumstances.

An important rule is 2.3; parties may be relieved from a failure to comply with the rules if due to mistake, oversight or other excusable cause.

The Summary Application must be raised in the sheriffdom where the property is situated and usually in the sheriff court district where the property is situated. The Sheriff has a wide discretion in deciding in how the appeal should proceed but should have regard for the summary nature of the procedure; Sheriff Courts (Scotland) Act 1907 S.50.

Ordinarily, the Summary Application should be returned to the court not later than 12 noon on the second working day before the first calling. It is unlikely that a Sheriff can determine applications under section 28 of the 2003 Act at first calling. The Sheriff will usually order answers and a period of adjustment up to an appointed date The Sheriff may order that record is lodged containing the parties' adjusted pleadings.

If a Summary Application is lacking in specification (e.g. the extent of the property in question) a Sheriff can competently assign a Debate. In certain circumstances the Sheriff can even sist proceedings.

At the end of any adjustment period the Sheriff will normally assign a Proof on the Summary Application where evidence is lead or agreed evidence is put before the court. Thereafter, the Sheriff will issue a formal written judgment.

An aggrieved party appeal the Sheriff's judgment to the Sheriff Appeal Court and does not require leave to do so. The appeal should be lodged with the Sheriff Appeal Court (S.A.C) within 28 days of the Sheriff's judgment. If a party remains aggrieved at any decision of the S.A.C. there can be a further Appeal to the Inner House of the S.A.C if the S.A.C permits this.

Time Limit

Rule 2.6 covers this:

"2.6—(1) *This rule applies to a summary application where the time within which the application may be made is not otherwise prescribed.*

(2) *An application to which this rule applies shall be lodged with the sheriff clerk within 21 days after the date on which the decision, order, scheme, determination, refusal or other act complained of was intimated to the pursuer.*

(3) *On special cause shown, the sheriff may hear an application to which this rule applies notwithstanding that it was not lodged within the period prescribed in paragraph (2)."*

CHAPTER THIRTEEN

CONCLUSION

As will be clear there were a number of cases litigated since the 2003 Act was enacted. Generally, the frequency and volume of these cases lessened as the principles of the 2003 Act were clarified. Anstalt is a very clear judgment and is easy to understand. In conclusion:

- The court should consider whether the land is covered by the provisions of the 2003 Act.

- Having done so do any section 6 exclusions apply? What happened before the 2003 Act, such as the erection of a fence, is immaterial. If an owner does or omits to do something the court will look at these acts or omissions objectively regardless of the intention of the owner.

- In determining issues under the 2003 Act there should be objective analysis as opposed to the *bona fide* subjective views of landowner. What would a court determine?

- Notices discouraging access or locked gates must be necessary with no reasonable alternative. If necessary, land owner should form a safe enclosed access from "A" to "B" where there are cattle (or wild boar!).

- The area of ground required for reasonable privacy cannot be extended by strategically placing structures such as children's play equipment or barbeque huts.

- With reference to section 6 (1) (iv) of the 2003 Act, see Gloag case, should security issues be a relevant consideration? The focus of the 2003 Act is "privacy" as opposed to "security". "Privacy" can be assessed objectively having regard to the location and type of the property. "Security" is particular to the individual or individuals living within the property. Anstalt does not appear to address this.

Happy roaming, owning, managing and don't distress the Adders.

APPENDIX ONE

SUMMARY APPLICATION
AND ANSWERS

FORM 1

SHERIFFDOM OF ANYWHERE AT ANYWHERE

RECORD

In the cause

SUMMARY APPLICATION IN TERMS OF SECTIONS 14(4) and 28 (1) (A) OF THE LAND REFORM (SCOTLAND) ACT 2003

by

ANDREW ANYONE AND AMANDA ANYONE, Spouses, residing together at Adder House, Adder Estate, Anywhere, AN1 9AN

PURSUERS

against

ANYWHERE COUNCIL, A Local Authority having its principal office at Council Castle, Anywhere, AN1 9AM

DEFENDER

The Pursuers crave the court-

1. To quash the notice served by Anywhere Council under and in terms of section 14 of the Land Reform (Scotland) Act 2003 on the pursuers on 4th January 2023 relating to a sign, which notice is annexed hereto as Appendix 1, in terms of section 14(4) of the Land Reform (Scotland) Act 2003 ("private road no public access")

2. To quash the notice served by Anywhere Council under and in terms of section 14 of the Land Reform (Scotland) Act 2003 on the pursuers on 4th January 2023 relating to a sign, which notice is annexed hereto as Appendix 2, in terms of section 14(4) of the Land Reform (Scotland) Act 2003; ("Adders-Keep out")

3. To quash the notice served by Anywhere Council under and in terms of the Land Reform (Scotland) Act 2003 on the pursuers on 4th January 2023 relating to removal of barbed wire from a gate which notice is annexed hereto as Appendix 2, in terms of section 14(4) of the Land Reform (Scotland) Act 2003.

4. To find and declare in terms of Section 28(1) of the Land Reform (Scotland) Act 2003 that the area of land belonging to the pursuers consisting of (i) that area of land registered in the Land Register for Scotland under Title number AN123; (ii) that area of land registered in the Land Register for Scotland under Title number ANY124; and (iii) that area of land more particularly described in and disponed by a Disposition by A Person in favour of the pursuers dated 30 June 1992, is land over which access rights are not exercisable pursuant to Sections 6(b)(iv) and, separatim, 6(1)(c) of the Land Reform(Scotland) Act 2003; and

5. To find the defenders liable to the Pursuer in the expenses of this Application.

STATEMENT OF FACTS FOR THE PURSUERS

and

ANSWERS thereto for the DEFENDERS

STAT. 1

The pursuers are spouses residing together at Adder House, Adder Estate, Anywhere, AN1 9AN. They are domiciled there. The defender is a Local Authority in which certain rights and duties are vested in terms of the Land Reform (Scotland) Act 2003 ("the Act"). The defender has its principal office at Council Castle, Anywhere, AN1 9AM. The present action has as its subject matter notices which have been issued by the defender in relation to land belonging to the pursuers at Adder Estate, Anywhere, which lies within this Sheriffdom. The present action also has as its subject matter the existence or otherwise of access rights over such land in terms of the Act. This court accordingly has jurisdiction.

ANS. 1

Admitted that the parties are as designed in the instance. Admitted that the pursuers are spouses residing together at Adder House, Adder Estate, Anywhere, AN1 9AN. Admitted that they are domiciled there. Admitted that the defender is a Local Authority in which certain rights and duties are vested in terms of the Land Reform (Scotland) Act 2003 ("the Act"). Admitted that the defender has its principal office at Council Castle, Anywhere, AN1 9AM. Admitted that the present action has as its subject matter notices which have been issued by the defender in relation to land belonging to the pursuers at Adder Estate, Anywhere which lies within this Sheriffdom. Admitted that the present action also has as its subject matter the existence or otherwise of access rights over such land in terms of the Act. Admitted that this court accordingly has jurisdiction.

STAT.2

To the knowledge of the pursuers, there are no proceedings pending before this or any other court involving the present cause of action between the parties hereto. To the knowledge of the pursuers, there is no agreement between the parties prorogating jurisdiction over the subject matter of the present cause to any other court. The defender's averments in answer are denied except insofar as coinciding herewith.

ANS. 2

Admitted that there are no proceedings pending before this or any other court involving the present cause of action between the parties hereto. Admitted there is no agreement between the parties prorogating jurisdiction over the subject matter of the present cause to any other court under explanation that there can be no such agreement. *Quoad ultra* denied.

STAT. 3

The pursuers are heritable proprietors of an area of land extending to approximately eight acres known as Adder Estate, Anywhere, AN1 9AN. It is rural property. The Title to their land comprises three contiguous parcels, namely (i) the area of land registered in the Land Register of Scotland under Title number ANY123, (ii) that area of land registered in the Land Register for Scotland under Title number ANY124; and (iii) that area of land more particularly described in and disponed by a Disposition by A Person in favour of the pursuers dated 30 June 1991. For the purposes of this application, these three parcels are collectively known as "the Estate". The area of land consisting of only Title number ANY 123 extends to approximately 3 acres and is known as "Adder House", and the area of land consisting of the other two parcels extends to approximately 5 acres and is known as "Adder Lodge". The Estate forms part of the larger area known as "Adder Land" which extends to approx. 10000 acres. Copies of the Pursuers' said titles are produced and are referred to for their terms. A copy of the plan for Adder Land is also produced showing areas (i), (ii) and (iii) of the pursuer's title edged in red and coloured pink, yellow and orange respectively on the said plan.

ANS.3

Admitted that the pursuers are heritable proprietors of an area of land extending to approximately eight acres being Adder Estate, Anywhere, AN1 9AN ("the Estate"). Admitted that the pursuers reside at Adder House. Admitted that Anywhere Estate is a rural property. Admitted that the title to their land comprises three contiguous parcels, namely (i) the area of land registered in the Land Register of Scotland under Title number ANY123, (ii) that area of land registered in the Land Register for Scotland under Title number ANY124; and (iii) that area of land more particularly described in and disponed by a Disposition by A Person in favour of the pursuers dated 30 June 1991. Admitted that for the purposes of this application, these three parcels are collectively known as "the Estate". Believed to be true that the area of land consisting of only Title number ANY 123 extends to approximately 3 acres and is known as "Adder House", and the area of land consisting of the other two parcels extends to approximately 5 acres and is known as "Adder Lodge". Believed to be true that the subjects form part of the larger area known as "Adder Land" which extended to approximately 10000 acres. The terms of the pursuers' titles are admitted. The coloured plan is referred to for its terms beyond which no admission is made. *Quoad ultra* denied

STAT.4

The pursuers purchased the Estate on or around 20 October 1992. Admitted that it includes a fifteen bedroom house (Adder House) dating back to the early 1500s, together with an area of land. It has previously been used as an Adder hunting lodge, a farmhouse and a substantial family home. Adder Lodge was purchased by the pursuers on or around

30 November 2012. It was the former lodge house of Anywhere Castle and sits at the bottom of the drive up to Adder House and Anywhere Castle being an adjacent property. It was bought by the pursuers as a business, and is currently in the process of extensive renovation to render it suitable for short-term holiday letting. The principal attraction of Adder Lodge for visitors is its privacy, peace, tranquillity and an abundance of beautiful snakes. It was let on an assured tenancy prior to and at the time the pursuers purchased it. It had been occupied more or less continuously previously. The land attaching to these properties extends in total to around 8 acres, which is long and relatively thin in nature, and which had originally been planned and laid out as garden ground for the adjacent Anywhere Castle. Its status as a private garden date back to the eighth and ninth centuries. It is not a large area having regard to the status of Anywhere Estate. From Adder House, it takes approximately 3 minutes to walk to the bottom boundary, 3 minutes to walk to the top boundary and 2 minutes to walk from one side of the subjects to the other. Within the garden area (but not within the Pursuers' Title) there is also a holiday cottage for the McAnyone family ("McAnyone Cottage) who bought part of the Estate in or around 1346. McAnyone Cottage is still extensively visited with the latest member of the McAnyone family staying there on January 1st 2023 for two weeks. The McAnyones' Family Trust, as owners of McAnyone Cottage ,have private rights of access over the pursuers' subjects in order to visit it. These rights are reflected within the pursuers' titles. With reference to the defender's averments in answer admitted that Anywhere Lodge lies within ten metres of the main M900 motorway with a core path running close to its eastern boundary and a public footpath running near to its western boundary. Admitted that McAnyone Cottage belongs to the McAnyone family (under explanation that it is, as hereinbefore averred, held in trust by the McAnyones' Family Trust.) *Quoad ultra* the defender's averments in answer are denied except insofar as coinciding herewith.

ANS. 4

Believed to be true that the pursuers purchased Adder Estate on or around 20 October 1992. Believed to be true that it comprises a fifteen bedroom detached house dating back to the early 1500's together with an area of land. Believed to be true that it has previously been used as a hunting lodge, a farmhouse and a substantial family home. Believed to be true that Adder Lodge was purchased by the pursuers on or around 30 November 2002. Believed to be true that it was a former lodge house of Anywhere Castle and sits at the bottom of the drive up to Anywhere House. Believed to be true that it was bought by the pursuers as a business and is in the process of extensive renovation to render it suitable for short term holiday letting. Believed to be true that it was let on an assured tenancy prior to and at the time that the pursuers purchased it and it had been occupied more or less continuously previously. Believed to be true that the land attaching to these properties extends in total to around 8 acres which is long and relatively thin in nature and which had originally been planned and laid out as a garden for the adjacent Anywhere Castle. Not known and not admitted that it takes approximately 2 minutes to walk from Adder House to the bottom boundary, 3 minutes to the top boundary and 2 minutes from one side of the subject to the other. Quoad ultra denied. Explained and averred that Adder Lodge lies within ten metres of the main M900 motorway with a core path running close to its eastern boundary and a public footpath running near to its western boundary. There is also McAnyone Cottage which is believed to belong to the McAnyone family. Explained and averred that the land surrounding McAnyone Cottage does not comprise any part of sufficient adjacent land to enable persons living in Anywhere House to have reasonable measures of privacy in that house and to ensure their enjoyment of that house is not unreasonably disturbed.

STAT.5

The subjects are broadly bounded by a river on one side and the M900 on the other. When the pursuers purchased Adder Estate and latterly Adder Lodge the garden area was completely overgrown and impenetrable, the main driveway to Adder House/Anywhere Castle was impassable and had not been in use for a period of approximately forty years. Indeed, historically that driveway had been used as access for Anywhere Castle but the access arrangements for the Castle were changed several decades ago, so that the driveway to Anywhere Estate only accesses Adder House and Adder Lodge. Any rights of access which existed previously had prescribed long before the pursuers purchased Adder Estate. There are no private rights of access over this driveway apart from the McAnywhere family, their invitees and one other limited exception. There are no parking facilities within the subjects apart from private parking (Anywhere House, Anywhere Lodge and for McAnyone Cottage). The defenders averments in answer are denied except insofar as coinciding herewith.

ANS.5

Admitted that the subjects are broadly bounded by a river on one side and the M900 on the other. Not known and not admitted that when the pursuers purchased Adder Estate and latterly Adder Lodge the garden area was completely overgrown and impenetrable, the main driveway to Anywhere Castle was impassable and had not been in use for approximately 40 years. Believed to be true that historically that driveway had been used for access for Anywhere Castle but the access arrangement for the Castle were changed several decades ago so that the driveway to Anywhere Castle only accesses Adder House and Adder Lodge. Believed to be true that there are no private rights of access over the driveway apart from those vested in the McAnyone family and one other limited exception. Believed to be true that there are no parking facilities within the subjects apart from for private parking as averred by the pursuers. *Quoad ultra* denied. Explained and averred that the absence or otherwise of parking rights within or private rights of access over the subjects are not material factors in determining whether or not access rights are exercisable in terms of Part 1 of the Land Reform (Scotland) Act 2003 ("the Act").

STAT.6

Whilst Adder House had previously been used as a farm as well as a hunting lodge, the pursuers bought it with the sole intention of using it as a family home and restoring its woodland gardens to their former glory for their own private use and enjoyment. It was purchased specifically because of the peace and privacy which the gardens afforded. To that end, in or around 2001 the driveway was reinstated by them and, in parts, rebuilt. The pursuers have a love of trees and were keen to reinstate the woodland garden. The pursuers and their predecessors in title appreciate the beauty of Adders. Over a period from the year 1993 to date, the pursuers have progressively been improving and tidying up the garden area. They have re-populated the subjects with Adders subsequent to a cull by local farmers in the 1970's. This area was originally laid out as an organised planted area for Anywhere Castle, but through years of neglect it had become badly overgrown, significant areas of it (including original paths) had been washed away, and in parts it had become impenetrable due to fallen trees, debris and self-seeded plants. During the course of this process, the pursuers have sought to restore the original form, they have removed many of the self-seeded plants and trees to allow the original specimens such as ferns to thrive once more, they have cleared blockages, they have replaced small bridges and culverts, and they have installed for themselves benches and a barbecue area. They have done all this for their private use and enjoyment, expending considerable sums of money in the process, and to enable Adders to thrive. They have, to promote a protected species and have installed rocks for Adders to rest under and sunbathe on. The Adders become distressed if startled by visitors with heavy foot prints. They have constructed Adder nests. They did not do so for the benefit of the general public, although on each and every occasion when they have been asked, they have permitted members of the public to walk round the garden to enjoy the views, visit the chapel of rest and to mingle with the Adders in their natural habitat. This has enabled interested people to enjoy the beauty and tranquillity of the garden, but in a controlled manner and subject to the Pursuers' discretion. In addition to these works, the Pursuers have also commenced construction of a garage for Adder House and patio area for Adder Lodge. On the site, there are shelters constructed for the storage of several thousand pounds worth of equipment including lawnmowers and other gardening implements. These items are not secured from theft, albeit that is not a concern where members of the public are not free to wander round. The defender's averments in answer are denied except insofar as coinciding herewith.

ANS.6

Believed to be true that whilst Adder House had previously been used as a farm as well as a hunting lodge, the pursuers bought it with the sole intention of using it as a family home and restoring its woodland gardens to their former glory for their own private use and enjoyment. Believed to be true that in addition to these works the pursuers have also commenced construction of a garage for Adder House and patio area for Adder Lodge. Believed to be true that there are shelters constructed for the storage for several thousand pounds worth of equipment including lawnmowers and other gardening implements. Not known and not admitted that these items are secured from theft ,albeit that is not a concern where members of the public are not free to wander around. Not known and not admitted that it was purchased specifically because of the peace and privacy the gardens afforded. Not known and not admitted to that end in or around 2001 the driveway was re-instated by them and in parts rebuilt. Not known and not admitted that the pursuers have a love of trees and were keen to re-instate the woodland gardens. Not known and not admitted that over a period the pursuers have progressively been improving and tidying up the garden area. Not known and not admitted that the area was originally laid out as an organised planted area for Anywhere Castle but through years of neglect had badly overgrown and significant areas of it had been washed away and in parts become impenetrable due to fallen trees, debris and self-seeded plants. Not known and not admitted that during the course of this process the pursuers have sought to restore the original form and have introduced many self-seeded plants and trees to allow the originally species, such as ferns, to thrive once more. Not known and not admitted that they have done this all for their own private use and enjoyment, spending considerable sums of money in the process. Not known and not admitted that they did not do so for the benefit of the general public although on each and every occasion when the have been asked they have permitted members of the public to walk round the garden to enjoy the views. Not known and not admitted that this enabled interested people to enjoy the beauty and tranquillity of the garden but in a controlled manner and subject to the pursuers discretion. *Quoad ultra* denied. Explained and averred that the pursuers' and their predecessors in title did not and do not have any interest in Adders. Believed and averred that "Adder Estate" refers to it traditionally being a natural habitat for Adders. The pursuers have intensively reared Adders to deter visitors.

STAT.7

On 11 January 2008, the defender served three formal notices on the pursuers. These notices required the removal of barbed wire from the top of a gate at the one extremity of the subjects, and additionally, required the removal of signs at the other extremity which reads "Private road no access without permission" and "Adders Keep Out". These notices are annexed hereto. The signs and the gate referred to were not erected by the pursuers. They were already in place before the Pursuers bought Adder Estate. It is both implicit and explicit within these notices that the defender consider that rights of access exist for members of the general public in terms of the Land Reform (Scotland) Act 2003. Indeed, on the plans appended to the notices, the defender makes clear its view that members of the public have rights of access up the full length of the driveway (except the last few metres where the drive abuts Adder House), and throughout all areas of the garden apart from (a) the garden ground immediately surrounding Adder Lodge (albeit members of the public are said to have access to an area of the garden of Adder House immediately adjacent, which overlooks Anywhere Lodge and affords the garden thereof no privacy whatsoever); (b) a small parcel of land immediately adjacent to Adder House extending to approximately 15-20 metres away from the gable wall of the house and its front porch and windows on the front elevation; and (c) a small area to the rear of the house which is currently and which has traditionally been used for commercial purposes. Such limited areas afford the pursuers and their guests / tenants in Adder Lodge no privacy at all, and are wholly inappropriate for houses the size and stature of Adder House and Adder Lodge. The access rights asserted by the defender will diminish the value of the subjects by £100,000. Reference is made to the privacy and diminution in value report prepared by A Hiss, Surveyor, dated 2nd January 2023 that is produced. With reference to the defender's averments in answer admitted that the defender entered into further correspondence and discussions with the pursuers in which they sought to have the wording of the signs changed or it removed and to have the barbed wire removed from the gate. Admitted that the pursuers refused to do so and the defenders served written notices on the pursuers in exercise of the powers conferred by section 14 of the Act. Sections 1, 6, 13 and 14 of the 2003 Act are referred to for their full terms beyond which no admission is made. Believed to be true that the defender was advised by a "member of the public" that signs had been put up beside the track close to Adder Lodge which read "Private road no access without permission" and "Adders keep out.". Admitted that barbed wire had been placed on top of a gate giving access to the subjects at their northern end. The owner of Anywhere Castle was "the member of the public" that made a complaint to the defender. Admitted that on receipt of this information, Mr Joseph Bloggs who is employed by the defender as an access officer and whose duties include upholding access rights wrote to the pursuers and visited the property. Not known and not admitted that following on from his visit the defender considered that the said signs and barbed wire were for the main purpose of preventing or deterring access to the land over which access rights were exercisable. Not known and not admitted that the defender formed this view having given consideration to the extent to which the land might comprise sufficient adjacent land to enable persons living in a house to have reasonable measures of privacy and to ensure that such persons enjoyment of that house is not unreasonably disturbed and as such would be land over which access rights would not be exercisable. Not known and not admitted that the defender had regard to the provisions of the Act and in particular the factors referred to in section 7 (5) in reaching its decision that the whole of the subjects did not comprise land over which access rights were not exercisable. Not known and not admitted that the defender considered that the track that ran past Adder Lodge whilst passing close to the said lodge house was land over which access rights were exercisable. Not known and not admitted that the defender considered that the location and characteristics of Adder Lodge were that it was a typical lodge house or gate house and as such would normally be expected to have an access way or driveway passing close to it and that anyone living there could reasonably expect persons to be passing by close to their house. Not known and not admitted that the defender also took account of the location of Adder Lodge being close to the M900. Not known and not admitted that the defender also considered the extent of sufficient adjacent land required to enable persons living in Adder House to have reasonable measures of privacy in that house and to ensure that their enjoyment of the house was not unreasonably disturbed. Not known and not admitted that whilst the defender recognised that there would be an area of ground surrounding Adder House over which access rights would not be exercisable that area was not so great that it extended as far as the gate on the northern boundary on which barbed wire had been placed nor did it extend as far as the said sign placed beside the track on the southern boundary. Not known and not admitted that in assessing the extent of the area surrounding Adder House over which access rights are not exercisable the defender had regard to the location and characteristics of the house and in particular its close proximity to a public road. The defender's averments in answer are denied except insofar as coinciding herewith.

ANS. 7

Admitted that on 11 January 2008 the defender served formal notices on the pursuers. Admitted that these notices required the removal of barbed wire from the top of a gate at the one extremity of the subjects and also required the removal of sig at the extremity which reads "Private Road No Access without Permission" and "Adders Keep Out". Quoad ultra denied. Explained and averred that in terms of section 1 of the Act everyone has the statutory rights established by Part 1 of the Act. These rights may only be exercised for the purposes set out in section 1 (3) and these purposes include recreational purposes and the carrying out of a relevant educational activity. The land in respect of which access rights are exercisable is all land except that specified or referred to under section 6 of the Act. Section 6 specifies inter alia that in relation to a house access rights are not exercisable over land which comprises sufficient adjacent land to enable persons living there to have reasonable measures of privacy in that house and to ensure that their enjoyment of that house is not unreasonably disturbed. Section 13 of the Act places a duty on a local authority to assert, protect and keep open and free from obstruction and encroachment any route, waterway or any other means by which access rights may reasonably be exercised. Section 14 (1) of the Act states that the owner of land in respect of which access rights are exercisable shall not inter alia put up any sign or notice or put up any fence or wall or take, or fail to take any other action for the main purpose of preventing or deterring any person entitled to exercise access rights from so doing. Where a local authority consider that anything has been done in contravention of section 14 (1) they may by written notice served on the owner of the land require that such remedial action as is specified in the notice be taken by the owner of the land within such reasonable time as is specified. In or around August 2006 the defender was advised by a member of the public that signs had been put up beside the track close to Adder Lodge which read "Private road no access without permission" and "Adders keep out". Barbed wire had been placed on top of a gate giving access to the subjects at their northern end. On receipt of this information Mr Joseph Bloggs who is employed by the defender as an access officer and whose duties include upholding access rights wrote to the pursuers and visited the property. Following on from his visit the defender considered that the said signs and barbed wire were for the main purpose of preventing or deterring access to land over which access rights were exercisable. The defender formed this view having given consideration to the extent to which the land might comprise sufficient adjacent land to enable persons living in a house to have reasonable measures of privacy and to ensure that such persons enjoyment of that house is not unreasonably disturbed and as such would be land over which access rights would not be exercisable. The defender had regard to the provisions of the Act and in particular the factors referred to in section 7 (5) in reaching its decision that the whole of the subjects did not comprise land over which access rights were not exercisable. The defender considered that the track that ran past Anywhere Lodge whilst passing close to the said lodge house was land over which access rights were exercisable. The defender considered that the location and characteristics of Adder Lodge were that it was a typical lodge house or gate house and as such would normally be expected to have an access way or driveway passing close to it and that anyone living there could reasonably expect persons to be passing by close to their house. The defender also took account of the location of Adder Lodge being close to the M900. The defender also considered the extent of sufficient adjacent land required to enable persons living in Adder House to have reasonable measures of privacy in that house and to ensure that their enjoyment of the house was not unreasonably disturbed. Whilst the defender recognised that there would be an area of ground surrounding Adder House over which access rights would not be exercisable that area was not so great that it extended as far as the gate on the northern boundary on which barbed wire had been placed nor did it extend as far as the said sign placed beside the track on the southern boundary. In assessing the extent of the area surrounding Adder House over which access rights are not exercisable the defender had regard to the location and characteristics of the house and in particular its close proximity to a public road. Further explained and averred that the defender entered into further correspondence and discussions with the pursuers throughout the period between September 2006 and early January 2008 in which they sought to have the wording of the signs changed or it removed and to have the barbed wire removed from the gate. The pursuers refused to do so and the defenders served written notices on the pursuers in exercise of the powers conferred by section 14 of the Act on 11 January 2008. With reference to the pursuers' averments regarding diminution in value not known and not admitted that there is any such diminution under explanation that it is not a relevant factor in determining this application.

STAT. 8

The pursuers object to there being unrestricted public rights of access over their entire garden. As hereinbefore condescended upon, the pursuers have never sought to prevent those who have asked from taking access, but they object to having members of the public having unrestricted access throughout their garden. Accordingly, they appeal against the issue of these notices and also respectfully invite the court to grant decree of declarator in terms of Sections 6 and 28 of the Land Reform (Scotland) Act 2003 excluding public rights of access from the subject. Specifically, and in addition to the general background hereinbefore condescended upon, the Pursuers rely on the following factors:-

(1) The pursuers reasonably estimate that if members of the public have

unrestricted rights of access over their property, the value thereof will be reduced by approximately £100,000.

(2) The pursuers purchased the subjects before the 2003 Act came into force, and in so doing, they purchased the subjects with the

specific view to enjoying the privacy which the gardens afforded. That privacy will be destroyed if members of the public have access.

(3) Adder House and Adder Lodge both include substantial and historic dwelling houses, with which one would expect a substantial and private garden. That ground does not require to be neatly laid out with lawn and flower bed in order to constitute garden ground. Whilst there is a grassy area in front of Adder House, the defender in its notices do not distinguish between that and any other type of ground and in any event, the majority of the garden consists of managed woodland. The fact that it is woodland does not make it any less of a garden.

(4) The pursuers have expended considerable sums of money in bringing this woodland area back to its former glory. They have done so for their benefit and to provide them with peace, tranquillity and privacy, which is why they purchased the subjects in the first place. The land conveyed to them is necessary for them to have such peace, privacy and tranquillity. They have repopulated the subjects with Adders. These benefits would all be absent if the notices issued by the defender. are upheld. This also comprises a work in progress, in respect that the pursuers still have considerably more work to do in order to finish their restoration project. That restoration will be prejudiced by public access.

(5) The pursuers have in the past encountered difficulties with people parking in the subjects in order to walk part of the nearby core path and such parking difficulties will only be exacerbated if members of the public are allowed to roam free through the subjects.

(6) The subjects also include fishing rights and if members of the public are permitted unrestricted access, the pursuers will not be able to enjoy the benefit of those rights without being disturbed.

(7)   The pursuers engage in a considerable amount of charitable activity and use the peace and tranquillity of their land for the purposes of thinking and quiet contemplation. This will be denied to them unless the notices are quashed.

(8)   The paths which the pursuers have uncovered in the course of their restoration are all original garden paths, and were not designed or built to accommodate any more than low volume private use. Consequently, if the public have unrestricted access, it is likely that even if people are exercising that access responsibly, the fabric of these old and fragile paths will be damaged. The pursuers have already had to replace a number of small bridges for their own use and many areas of the path are currently impassable because of drainage problems. This does not matter when the area is not being heavily trafficked, but it will lead to degradation of the area if the subjects suffer heavy pedestrian traffic.

(9)   The pursuers have concerns over security. As hereinbefore condescended upon, they store thousands of pounds worth of machinery in the Subjects, which is used for the maintenance and upkeep of the subjects as well as for their restoration. This equipment is not secured except by the fact that it is hidden from the public gaze. They recently had a substantial gas barbecue stolen. A number of Adders have been stolen including "Andy" their beloved pet Adder. The pursuers also have concerns about their own personal security and have already encountered persons unknown looking through the windows of Adder House. Such concerns will justifiably be heightened if members of the public are free to pass throughout the pursuers' private and undisturbed garden, and this would almost inevitably lead to thefts, vandalism and anti-social behaviour. It would be impossible to police these areas in such a remote and quiet area. The pursuers should not be subjected to such risks.

ANS. 8

Believed to be true that the pursuers object to there being unrestricted access over their entire garden. Believed to be true that the pursuers have never sought to prevent those who have asked from taking access. Quad ultra denied. Explained and averred that the access rights established by Part 1 of the Act entitle members of the public to exercise responsible access for the purposes set out in section 1 (3) of the Act without any requirement to notify the landowner or seek consent. Further explained and averred with specific reference to the factors set out by the Pursuers in sub paragraphs numbered (1) to (9) of paragraph 8 of their Statements of Facts (following the Pursuers' numbering):

1. Any apprehended or actual diminution in the value of property is not relevant to the question of the extent of rights of public access under the 2003 Act. Nor is apprehended distress to Adders.

2. The date when the property was purchased in relation to the coming into force of the 2003 Act and the purpose for which the property was purchased are not relevant to a consideration of the extent of public rights of access. In relation to the pursuers averment that their privacy will be destroyed if members of the public have access (which is denied) the defender accepts that the pursuers are entitled to prevent or deter public access to land which comprises sufficient adjacent land to the house of Adder House to enable persons living there to have reasonable measures of privacy. Explained and averred however that such land as comprises sufficient adjacent land for this purpose does not however extend as far as the sign and the gate in respect of which the defenders have served notices under section 14 of the Act.

3. The extent of the area of ground that may be considered garden ground is not a determining factor in deciding whether or not access rights are exercisable. In relation to a house access rights are not exercisable over land which comprises sufficient adjacent land to enable persons living there to have reasonable measures

of privacy in that house and to ensure that their enjoyment of that house is not unreasonably disturbed.

4. The matters referred to by the pursuers are only relevant in so far as they may assist in determining whether any part of the subjects falls within the categories of land over which access rights are not exercisable as set out in section 6 of the Act.

5. Explained and averred that access rights under the Act do not include vehicular rights of access and that public access to the subjects would not confer any right to park vehicles.

6. Section 2 of the Act states that a person only has access rights if they are exercised responsibly. The Scottish Outdoor Access Code ("the Code") gives guidance as to the circumstances in which those exercising rights are to be regarded as doing so in a way which is not responsible. Explained and averred that anyone exercising responsible access to the subjects and having regard to the advice set out in the Code would respect the interests of other people, would act with courtesy and consideration and respect the needs of other people enjoying the outdoors and in so doing would not cause unnecessary disturbance to persons fishing. Said Code is produced.

7. The matters referred to are only relevant in so far as they have a bearing on the extent to which land may be exempt from access rights under section 6 of the Act.

8. The matters referred to are not relevant to a determination of the extent to which access rights are exercisable.

9. Access rights do not extend to any building or structure or works, plant or fixed machinery. Access rights are not exercisable over land which forms the curtilage of a building which is not a house. Access rights are not exercisable over land which comprises sufficient adjacent land to enable persons living there to have

reasonable measures of privacy in that house and to ensure that their enjoyment of that house is not unreasonably disturbed. Explained and averred that allowing members of the public to exercise responsible access over those parts of the subjects which do not fall within any of the exempt areas referred to in section 6 of the act will not inevitably lead to thefts, vandalism and anti-social behaviour. Not known and not admitted that "Andy" the pursuers' pet Adder has been stolen.

STAT. 9

The pursuers have sought to persuade the defender that the subjects ought to be excluded from the scope of section 1 of the Land Reform (Scotland) Act 2003 but (notwithstanding that the Defender's Access Officer appears to agree that the pursuers will lose their privacy), the defender insists on proceeding and accordingly, this action is necessary. The defender's averments in answer are denied except insofar as coinciding herewith.

ANS.9

Denied. Explained and averred that there are parts of the subjects over which access rights in terms of Part 1 of the Act are not exercisable. These areas comprise sufficient adjacent land to enable persons living in Adder Lodge and Adder House respectively to have reasonable measures of privacy in each house respectively and to ensure that their enjoyment of that house is not unreasonably disturbed. Explained and averred that having regard to the characteristics and location of Anywhere Lodge, namely a typical gatehouse or lodge house situated within 50 metres of the M900 where the residents could reasonably expect vehicles and pedestrians to use the access track passing the front of the property then the said access track should not be regarded as sufficient adjacent land to enable persons living there to have reasonable measures of privacy in that house and to ensure that their enjoyment of that house is not unreasonably disturbed. The sign erected by the pursuers close to Adder Lodge has as its main purpose the deterrence of persons entitled to exercise access rights on said track and is therefore contravening the terms of section 14 of the Act and should be removed or reworded in such a way that it does not deter those who would seek to exercise responsible access. Further explained and averred that those persons living in Adder House are entitled to prevent or deter access to sufficient adjacent land for the purposes of privacy and enjoyment of the house as set out in section 6(1) (b) (iv) of the Act but that this area does not extend as far as the said sign or to the said gate with barbed wire on it to the north. The main purpose of the barbed wire on the said gate is to prevent or deter access and it therefore contravenes section 14 of the Act and should be removed. Further explained and averred that included in the factors which go to determine what extent of land is sufficient for the purposes of section 6 (1) (b) (iv) are the location and other characteristics of Adder Lodge. Explained and averred that although Adder House has the characteristics of a fairly substantial detached house in the countryside it is situated no more than 50 metres from the M900. Further explained averred that the land around the McAnyones' Lodge is not land in respect of which access rights are not exercisable by virtue of section 6 (1) (b) (iv) of the Act. Further explained and averred that the said sign and barbed wire have the purpose of preventing or deterring access to the entire subjects and as such the defender was entitled to serve said notices under section 14. Explained and averred that the public are entitled to take access to the subjects with the exception of those areas hereinbefore condescended upon. The said notices should be upheld.

PLEAS-IN-LAW for PURSUERS

1.   In the circumstances, it is appropriate for the court to grant decree of declarator in terms of Sections 6 and 28 of the said Act and the notices issued by the Defenders should be quashed accordingly.

IN RESPECT WHEREOF

Vipera Berus

Solicitor

Anywhere LLP

6 Snakes and Adders Square

Anywhere

AW96 4AD

SOLICITOR FOR PURSUERS

PLEAS-IN-LAW for DEFENDER

1. The entire subjects not being land in respect of which access rights are not exercisable decree of declarator should not be pronounced as craved.

2. The Pursuers having put up a sign and having placed barbed wire on a fence the main purpose of which is to prevent or deter the public from exercising their statutory right of access as established by Part 1 of the Land Reform (Scotland) Act 2003 the Notices served by the Defenders on the Pursuers under section 14 of the Act should be upheld.

3. The pursuers' averments anent (i) diminution in value, and (ii) distress to Adders being irrelevant they should not be admitted to probation.

IN RESPECT WHEREOF

Andriana Adder

Solicitor

Anywhere Council

Council Castle

Anywhere

AN1 9AM

SOLICITOR FOR DEFENDERS

MORE BOOKS BY
LAW BRIEF PUBLISHING

A selection of our other titles available now:-

'A Practical Guide to Parental Alienation in Private and Public Law Children Cases' by Sam King QC & Frankie Shama
'Contested Heritage – Removing Art from Land and Historic Buildings' by Richard Harwood QC, Catherine Dobson, David Sawtell
'The Limits of Separate Legal Personality: When Those Running a Company Can Be Held Personally Liable for Losses Caused to Third Parties Outside of the Company' by Dr Mike Wilkinson
'A Practical Guide to Transgender Law' by Robin Moira White & Nicola Newbegin
'Artificial Intelligence – The Practical Legal Issues (2nd Edition)' by John Buyers
'A Practical Guide to Residential Freehold Conveyancing' by Lorraine Richardson
'A Practical Guide to Pensions on Divorce for Lawyers' by Bryan Scant
'A Practical Guide to Challenging Sham Marriage Allegations in Immigration Law' by Priya Solanki
'A Practical Guide to Legal Rights in Scotland' by Sarah-Jane Macdonald
'A Practical Guide to New Build Conveyancing' by Paul Sams & Rebecca East
'A Practical Guide to Defending Barristers in Disciplinary Cases' by Marc Beaumont
'A Practical Guide to Inherited Wealth on Divorce' by Hayley Trim
'A Practical Guide to Practice Direction 12J and Domestic Abuse in Private Law Children Proceedings' by Rebecca Cross & Malvika Jaganmohan
'A Practical Guide to Confiscation and Restraint' by Narita Bahra QC, John Carl Townsend, David Winch
'A Practical Guide to the Law of Forests in Scotland' by Philip Buchan
'A Practical Guide to Health and Medical Cases in Immigration Law' by Rebecca Chapman & Miranda Butler
'A Practical Guide to Bad Character Evidence for Criminal Practitioners by Aparna Rao
'A Practical Guide to Extradition Law post-Brexit' by Myles Grandison et al

'A Practical Guide to Equity Release for Advisors' by Paul Sams
'A Practical Guide to Financial Services Claims' by Chris Hegarty
'The Law of Houses in Multiple Occupation: A Practical Guide to HMO Proceedings' by Julian Hunt
'Occupiers, Highways and Defective Premises Claims: A Practical Guide Post-Jackson – 2nd Edition' by Andrew Mckie
'A Practical Guide to Financial Ombudsman Service Claims' by Adam Temple & Robert Scrivenor
'A Practical Guide to Advising Schools on Employment Law' by Jonathan Holden
'A Practical Guide to Running Housing Disrepair and Cavity Wall Claims: 2nd Edition' by Andrew Mckie & Ian Skeate
'A Practical Guide to Holiday Sickness Claims – 2nd Edition' by Andrew Mckie & Ian Skeate
'Arguments and Tactics for Personal Injury and Clinical Negligence Claims' by Dorian Williams
'A Practical Guide to Drone Law' by Rufus Ballaster, Andrew Firman, Eleanor Clot
'A Practical Guide to Compliance for Personal Injury Firms Working With Claims Management Companies' by Paul Bennett
'RTA Allegations of Fraud in a Post-Jackson Era: The Handbook – 2nd Edition' by Andrew Mckie
'RTA Personal Injury Claims: A Practical Guide Post-Jackson' by Andrew Mckie
'On Experts: CPR35 for Lawyers and Experts' by David Boyle
'An Introduction to Personal Injury Law' by David Boyle

These books and more are available to order online direct from the publisher at www.lawbriefpublishing.com, where you can also read free sample chapters. For any queries, contact us on 0844 587 2383 or mail@lawbriefpublishing.com.

Our books are also usually in stock at www.amazon.co.uk with free next day delivery for Prime members, and at good legal bookshops such as Wildy & Sons.

We are regularly launching new books in our series of practical day-to-day practitioners' guides. Visit our website and join our free newsletter to be kept informed and to receive special offers, free chapters, etc.

You can also follow us on Twitter at www.twitter.com/lawbriefpub.

www.ingramcontent.com/pod-product-compliance
Lightning Source LLC
Chambersburg PA
CBHW030836210326
41598CB00049B/3486